# A Bit About Britain's High Days and Holidays

Mike Biles

In Memory of Dad
Kenneth John Biles
1916-1973
Who gave me my love of quirky things

By the same author
A Bit About Britain's History

# CONTENTS

# INTRODUCTION

'A Bit About Britain's High Days and Holidays' is another by-product of the A Bit About Britain website.

A High Day is a festival, a celebration; 'high' in this context means 'grand', or 'great'. The expression dates back to the English of the Middle Ages, at least, and will be found in the King James Bible (John xix. 31). A Holiday, of course, was originally a holy day, *halig daeg* in Old English, a saint's day or other religious festival. These days, 'holiday' usually just means a day, or days, off. The delightfully alliterative phrase 'High Days and Holidays' seems to be of British origin and was certainly in use in Victorian times. It simply refers to special occasions. Special occasions and holidays can be local in nature, of course, a prime example being Glasgow Fair, which began in the 12th century and developed into a holiday, when factories, shipyards and other businesses closed for a fortnight. Even a family may have its own high days and holidays; a notable anniversary perhaps, or a homecoming after a long absence. The author David Lodge mentions a particular room in a house, the front room or 'lounge', being rarely used "except on high days and holidays". I can relate to that. A Bit About Britain's High Days and Holidays attempts to describe traditional events in our nationally collective calendar that necessitate opening up lounges across the land, or perhaps taking to the streets, for.

When you get down to it, despite the secular and multi-cultural nature of modern Britain, most of our high days and holidays have religious roots. And that's simply because we are a product of our history, in which religion has played such a huge part. The year used to revolve around feast days of one sort or another and, to a great extent, still does; the academic year, for example, is largely dictated by Christmas and Easter. Religious association is not limited to Christian traditions, however, because alternative roots lurk behind many of the holy days we all know and love.

Some customs, inevitably, have declined in importance and have therefore been excluded from 'High Days and Holidays'. A prime example is May Day, a spring festival with roots at least as old as the ancient Celtic celebration of the coming of summer, Beltane, the fire of the god *Bel*. In Britain, May Day festivities had associations with the Green Man, or Robin Hood; there was Morris dancing, a May Queen and – of course – the May Pole. Though still celebrated in places, May Day is, sadly, no longer widely marked in modern Britain – though the Early May Bank Holiday is a reminder of it. Perhaps you'd like to revive it? Traditions evolve. If a version of this book were to be produced sometime in the distant future, it will feature different special occasions, and different details about any that are still marked. Perhaps Diwali, Yom Kippur, or Eid will be more widely celebrated. Any suggestions for prospective holidays of the future? Black Friday, maybe?

The final section of the book is an extensive list, by season, of annual events that normally take place in Britain, including sporting competitions and flower shows, along with our high days and holidays. Never again will you have any excuse to forget Rutland Day. It's always useful to have things like that handy, don't you think?

# BRITAIN

'Britain is an island in the North Atlantic, off the coast of western Europe. It is the largest of a group of about 6,000 islands (somebody took a boat out and counted them), collectively referred to as the British Isles – a geographical term. The island of Britain contains the nations of England, Wales, and Scotland. The three nations together form a political entity, Great Britain, which also includes several islands belonging to those nations. 'Great Britain' is commonly abbreviated to simply 'Britain', but both terms are used in a geographical as well as a political sense.

The nations of Great Britain are part of a sovereign state which includes Northern Ireland. This is the United Kingdom, or 'UK' - full name 'the United Kingdom of Great Britain and Northern Ireland'.

The UK is home to some 65 million souls, of which roughly 54 million live in England, 5.4 million in Scotland, 3.1 million in Wales and 1.9 million in Northern Ireland.

The inhabitants of Britain and the United Kingdom are generally referred to as 'British', or specifically from their country of origin – English, Scottish, Welsh or Northern Irish.

# 1
# PUBLIC HOLIDAYS

In Britain, there is little practical difference between a public or a bank holiday, and the terms are used interchangeably. A bank holiday is a legal holiday on a weekday when banks, schools and other institutions are closed. In theory, businesses close – but an increasing number now stay open, especially in the retail sector. Bank holidays can affect travel – for example, public transport companies often operate Sunday services and traffic on roads is often heavier. If a bank holiday date falls over a weekend, a substitute weekday – usually the next Monday - becomes the Bank Holiday. The Government occasionally changes Bank Holiday dates, or introduces a one-off holiday for a special event.

## SPRING HOLIDAYS
17 March – **St Patrick's Day** (N Ireland)

**Good Friday** and **Easter** Monday

May – the first Monday is **Early May Bank Holiday**

May – the last Monday is **Spring Bank Holiday**

## SUMMER HOLIDAYS
12 July – **Orangemen's Day** (N Ireland)

August – the first Monday is **Summer Bank Holiday** (Scotland)

August – the last Monday is late **Summer Bank Holiday** (England and Wales)

## AUTUMN HOLIDAYS
30 November – **St Andrew's Day** (Scotland)

## WINTER HOLIDAYS

24 December **Christmas Eve** – not a holiday, but many businesses close early

25 December – **Christmas Day**

26 December – **Boxing Day**

31 December – **New Year's Eve** – not a holiday, but many businesses close early

1 January – **New Year's Day**

2 January – **Scottish Bank Holiday**

# 2
# NEW YEAR'S DAY
## 1 January

 This seems as good a place as any to start. Janus, the two-faced Roman god of gates and beginnings, who gave his name to January, looks back on the old year and forward into the new. So, you'll be telling yourself that things will be better, that you're going to drink less, exercise more, read a book a week and give up smoking. If you've already done all of those things, you have nothing to look forward to.

1st January is the start of the new year in the Gregorian calendar, the most widely used calendar in the world. But it wasn't always that way. For one thing, Britain used to use the Julian calendar, which had been introduced by Julius Caesar in 46BC and which added two new months, January and February, to the old Roman year. Even then, New Year's Day was not always on 1st January and has in the past been marked on Christmas and Easter Days. In Medieval Britain, New Year's Day used to be on 25th March, Lady Day, the Feast of the Annunciation. January 1st was only established as the official start of the new year in Scotland in 1600 and in the rest of Britain in 1752. This was when Britain switched from the Julian calendar, which was inaccurate by about 18 hours every century, to the Gregorian calendar. The latter was introduced by Pope Gregory in 1582 and rectified the discrepancy, but Protestant Britain held off making the switch until 1752, by which time we were 11 days adrift from the rest of Western Europe. That year, 3rd September was renamed 14th September and a lot of folk felt aggrieved that someone had misappropriated 11 days of their lives.

New Year celebrations vary in nature across Britain, though since the late 20th century they have become more widespread, and extravagant. Festivities tend to take place mainly on New Year's Eve. The day itself is not a holiday, but many businesses close early, with parties being held in the evening over the countdown to midnight, when many listen for the chimes of Big Ben over the radio or TV. Church bells are rung and ships blow their horns. The opening minutes of the new year are invariably marked by the singing of Robbie Burns' Scots' song, 'Auld Lang Syne'. The phrase *auld lang syne* roughly means 'for old times' sake', and the song is a sentimental one about friendship and having a drink or three with old friends. The first verse and chorus are:

*Should auld acquaintance be forgot,*
*And never brought to mind?*
*Should auld acquaintance be forgot,*
*And auld lang syne.*
Chorus:
*For auld lang syne, my jo,*
*For auld lang syne,*
*We'll tak a cup o' kindness yet,*
*For auld lang syne.*

There are varying versions - and at least another four verses.

Although it is an international event, there is certainly something Scottish about New Year in Britain – or Hogmanay as it's known north of the border. And there are a couple of good reasons for that. Firstly, Hogmanay is a very old and established celebration in Scotland, with obscure roots: some say it has old Norse origins, others that it is French; some believe it dates back to pagan times. Secondly, since the Reformation of the 16th century, the fiercely Presbyterian Church of Scotland strongly discouraged the celebration of Christmas, which it saw as a frivolous Roman Catholic feast. So, for centuries the big mid-winter festival in Scotland was Hogmanay. New Year's Day has been a Bank Holiday in Scotland since 1871, but had to wait until 1974 before being made a Bank Holiday in England and Wales. 25th December, Christmas Day, on the other hand, only became a public holiday in Scotland in 1958. When New Year's Day became a holiday in England and Wales, Scotland was given additional holidays on 2nd January – as well as the day after Christmas, Boxing Day.

New Year traditions include 'first footing' – the first person to step over the threshold after midnight. This is said to be a Scottish tradition, although I remember it as one of the few markers of New Year as a boy in the south of England. For good luck, ideally the first footer should be a tall, dark, handsome individual, bearing coal for warmth in the cold of winter. Others say s/he should bring salt, bread and a dram of whisky too, symbols of wealth and food; not sure what the whisky represents, but it sounds like a great idea. To avoid the disappointment (or bad luck) of no one appearing, a member of the household may be shoved out the back door, clutching a lump of coal, with instructions to make their way to the front and knock for entry. Other traditions include taking out the ashes from the fire, or cleaning the house, to start the year afresh. It's bad luck to clean on New Year's Day, though. In Scottish homes, the furniture would be pushed back, rugs taken up and people would dance.

New Year's Day can be a time of recovery for many. Others mark the occasion with a public swim. In Scotland, it is common to socialise in people's homes, where steak pie may be served.

Away from the partying and the fireworks that have become part of New Year in many towns in modern Britain, it is worth mentioning a couple of more unusual celebrations. In the Aberdeenshire town of Stonehaven, the annual Fireballs Festival sees 40 or so residents parading up and down the High Street, swinging fiercely flaming balls around their heads. And in the Northern English town of Allendale is the Allendale Baal Festival, a fire festival in which whisky barrels filled with burning hot tar are carried in procession on the heads of 'guisers' – people in disguise.

For most of us, however, New Year is all about those resolutions.

# 3
# BURNS' NIGHT
## 25 January

Burns' Night is a celebration of prolific poet and lyricist Robert – Robbie or 'Rabbie' – Burns. Shakespeare, Chaucer, Dickens and Austen do not get their own annual supper event, but Burns does. He is Scotland's favourite bard, still revered throughout the land, indeed the world over, by those of Scottish descent as well as by many non-Scots. Each New Year, people sing (or mumble) the words of Auld Lang Syne, which Burns wrote in 1788. Of course, his detractors might argue that it's all a bit over the top, that Robbie Burns produced gushings of over-emotional verse that is, to most modern English-listeners, barely comprehensible, because the fellow wrote in *Lallans*, 'the guid Scots tongue'. Burns, his scathing doubters might go on to say, was too fond of drink and a good time, factors contributing to his early demise at the age of 37, having allegedly fathered a hoard of children to a variety of different women along the way. Now, as a proud and cynical *Sassenach, I offer some advice: if you're ever invited to a traditional Burns' Night, do not hesitate to accept.

Let's look into Robbie Burns, his life, works, places associated with him – and the essentials of a Burns' Night.

### Brief Burns' biography

Robert Burns was born on 25th January 1759, in a two-roomed thatched cottage built by his father, William, in the village of Alloway, in south-west Scotland. William Burnes (it had two syllables, 'burn-ess') was a gardener who married Agnes Broun (Brown) when he was in his late thirties and she about ten years younger. Robert was their first child and was joined by three brothers and three sisters. He wrote, "I was born a very poor man's son," which was entirely true; but that poor man saw to it that Robert had a surprisingly good education – partly at home, partly from a teacher William hired (sharing the cost with a neighbour) and partly at local schools. From his mother, Burns learned traditional tales and songs; his imagination was also influenced by a distant relative, Betty Davidson, who helped about the place.

> "She had, I suppose, the largest collection in the country of tales and songs concerning devils, ghosts, fairies, brownies, witches, warlocks, spunkies, kelpies, elf-handles, deadlights, wraiths, apparitions, cantraips, giants, enchanted towers, dragons and other trumpery."

William Burnes took on the lease of a farm and Robert continued his academic education while he was working, reading while walking, or driving his cart. It was a tough life and it seems his father was unlucky with the deals he made. When William died in 1784, worn down by debt and dispute with his landlord, Robert became head of the family.

Somehow, despite the difficulties the family had, Robert found the time and money to attend dancing classes in nearby Tarbolton and, with a group of friends, founded a Bachelors' Club (its meeting place is now a museum), the rules of which stated that:

> "Every man proper for a member of this Society must have a frank, honest, open heart; above anything dirty or mean; and must be a professed lover of one or more of the female sex."

You can't help being drawn by Burns' idealised, albeit often fickle, fascination with women. He immortalised many of the objects of his affection in verse; however, not all of his associations had happy endings. At fifteen, he fell in love for the first time, with Nelly Kilpatrick, 'Handsome Nell'. Next, he was smitten by Peggy Thompson, a "charming Fillette", who lived next door to the school he attended in Kirkoswald. He later blamed love for turning him into a poet, writing that rhyme and song became, "in a manner, the spontaneous language of my heart." In 1784, he had a romance with the family farm-servant, Elizabeth Paton (allegedly plain, but with a good figure), who gave birth to his daughter, Elizabeth. That same year, he met his future wife, Jean Armour, who fell pregnant in 1786 but whose parents disapproved of the penniless Robert – despite his avowed intention to marry their daughter. Thinking Jean had spurned him (so the story goes), Robert had an affair with a Mary Campbell, 'Highland Mary', who he also proposed to and who he tried to persuade to emigrate with him to the West Indies. Tragically, Mary died – possibly of typhoid, though some say in childbirth. Jean Armour went on to give birth to twins.

Meanwhile, Burns had just had the first volume of his poems published, in Kilmarnock. Known as 'the Kilmarnock Edition', 'Poems, Chiefly in the Scottish Dialect' had a print-run of 612 copies and sold out within a month. Burns went to Edinburgh, where he mixed with the society of the day and became known as 'the ploughman poet' – a rustic image the well-educated Burns often played up to. He travelled, in Scotland and northern England, met up again with Jean Armour, proposed to a Margaret Chalmers (who rejected him in favour of a banker – probably a more reliable prospect), fell in love with an Edinburgh society lady, Agnes McLehouse, and managed to make her maid, Jenny Clow, pregnant. Jenny gave birth to son and subsequently died, destitute, in 1792; it is not clear what happened to the boy. Agnes – also known as Nancy and, in correspondence with Burns, 'Clarinda' to his 'Sylvander' – is remembered in the lovely 'Ae Fond Kiss'.

Somehow, Burns found the time to begin contributing to

'The Scots Musical Museum', a collection of old songs which eventually ran to 6 volumes published between 1787 and 1803. This was a far-sighted project and Robert Burns' contribution to it was considerable, including original pieces as well as new lyrics for old tunes. Among the best known are 'Auld Lang Syne' (which Burns built on earlier versions of), 'My love is like a Red, Red Rose', 'Scots Wha Hae', 'Ye Banks and Braes of Bonnie Doon', 'Ae Fond Kiss', 'The Winter it is Past' and 'Comin' Thro the Rye'.

Burns, spending more than he earned, returned to Ayrshire and farming in 1788, and married Jean Armour; ultimately, they had nine children together. Farming didn't work for Rabbie, however, and he successfully contrived to be appointed as the local Excise Officer, or tax collector – which paid better. This work took him to Dumfries, where he and Jean went to live. Somewhere along the way, our man apparently had a fling with a young barmaid, Ann Park, at his favourite 'howff' (haunt, pub), the Globe Inn; Ann also fell pregnant and it seems she died, but that Jean took in the baby, Betty.

There has been some speculation about the cause of Burns' early death. Some, particularly those of the extreme life is no-fun brigade, have indeed blamed it all on the poet's libertine lifestyle. Certainly, Burns enjoyed a drink – and we have also seen that he indulged in what he might himself have called a little houghmagandy on occasion. Fortunately, though, these things aren't necessarily killers. However, there is no doubt that Burns was very ill for some time – and knew he was going to die. Modern experts suggest that he had suffered rheumatic fever as a youngster and that this resulted in bacterial endocarditis, leading to terminal heart failure. He died at home in Dumfries on 21st July 1796, in debt, and on the same day that Jean Armour gave birth to their last son, Maxwell. Thousands of people attended his funeral.

## Robert Burns' works

Now, I should first say that I claim no literary expertise whatsoever; secondly, I just didn't get Burns when I was at school. It is easy to dismiss something you don't understand, especially if you're fundamentally lazy. And, after all, Scotland has produced other great writers whose stuff isn't such a struggle to read if you don't happen to speak Scots – JM Barrie, John Buchan, Arthur Conan Doyle, Alistair MacLean, Walter Scott, Robert Louis Stevenson and Ian Rankin, to mention a few. Given the incredibly rich pool of poets and literary giants that the British Isles as a whole has produced, what is so special about someone who wrote in an apparently excruciating patois and whose brain appears to have been a periscope for his willie?

Burns wasn't with us long: he didn't make it to his 3 score years and 10; not even to his naughty forties. Yet he is internationally venerated. And this isn't a recent thing, grown out of some myth, popularised because of some faux historical movie, or because the head of marketing at the Scottish Nationalist Party wanted to create a hero – Scotland's got plenty of those. Nor was Burns like one of those old masters, scratching around during his lifetime and only receiving recognition years after he'd gone to a larger canvas in the sky. No, Burns achieved love, respect and regard when he was very much alive. And the clincher is that he did it in less than 10 years: he published his first book of poems, the Kilmarnock edition, when he was 27; a decade later, he was dead; this is a man to be reckoned with.

Not only did Burns have an extraordinary creative output in his short life; the themes he chose had universal appeal. He wrote about nature, hardship, patriotism – and, of course, romance. He could be hard-hitting; but also humorous and satirical. It seems to me he was acutely observational, rather like a modern stand-up comedian; an early Billy Connolly. And, like Connolly, he was a wonderfully intelligent man. The world was, of course, a very different place in the 18th century and Britain was going through a period of intense change. Interestingly, though some of Burns' work is very much of its time – for example, he clearly dislikes the fire and brimstone branch of the Church of Scotland and had Jacobite sympathies as well as contradictory radical ones - so much of what he writes is ageless; once you've worked your way through the guid auld Scots tongue.

There have been – and still are – many varieties of English. The lowland Scots of Robert Burns is one of them, with roots in the language spoken by the Anglian invaders of Northumbria, heavily spiced with other influences – not least Norse and Gaelic. There are still distinct varieties of English throughout the British Isles – dialects, if you like - though, sadly in many ways, there have always been good reasons to conform to a common standard, so the differences are being levelled - and language constantly evolves. It probably didn't help the Scots language that James VI of Scotland also became James I of England, or that he ordered every church in Scotland to use his Authorised Version of the Bible. By the 18th century, many in Scotland were keen to imitate the influential English of the south. But Burns, who was familiar with all the literary greats and perfectly capable of both speaking and writing the formal English of the day, chose to write in the traditional language of his land, the land that he knew, and thus made a powerful statement about Scottish culture. Burns was an undoubted patriot. Anyway, no Englishman worthy of his heritage has a problem with *"Whan that Aprile with his shoures soote"* – and some things are just better the way they are meant to be. Here's the first verse of Burns' poem 'To A Mouse', with an English version next to it:

| | |
|---|---|
| *Wee, sleekit, cowrin', tim'rous beastie* | *Little sleek, cowering, timorous creature* |
| *Oh, what a panic's in thy breastie!* | *Oh, what a panic's in your little breast!* |
| *Thou needna start away sa hasty,* | *You need not start away so hastily,* |
| *Wi' bick'ring brattle.* | *With hurried rush!* |
| *I wad be laith to rin and chase thee* | *I should be loath to run and chase you* |
| *Wi' murdering pattle!* | *With murdering plough-staff!* |

It strikes me that the original has a degree of power, whereas the English version is too twee for words. Hang on, though - it's about a mouse. Who writes a poem about a mouse?! Well, young Burns had disturbed this small beastie while he was working in a field, and the experience touched him. This guy had sensitivity. He not only wrote as people spoke, but he also wrote from the heart; it's impossible not to warm to him. Then there's his honesty; Burns had no time for hypocrites and, it seems, few illusions about himself:

*There's ae wee faut they whyles lay to me,*
*I like the lasses – Gude forgie me!*
*For monies a plack they wheedle frae me*
*At dance or fair;*
*Maybe some ither things they gie me*
*They weel can spare.*

From 'Epistle to J Lapraik'. Self-deprecation is an attractive quality; and you can almost see the twinkle in the eyes behind his words.

Lieutenant-Colonel Winston Churchill wrote to his wife Clem requesting a volume of Burns' poetry with which to "soothe and cheer" the spirits of his men, the 6th Royal Scots Fusiliers, serving with him in the filth and terror of the Western Front in 1916. Churchill thought, and I have to agree, that Burns would be as likely to lift his men as anything:

*Now's the day and now's the hour.*

From 'Scots Wha Hae' (Robert Bruce's march to Bannockburn). And, in contrast:

*Then come sweet muse inspire my lay!*
*For a' the lee lang Simmer's day*
*I couldna sing, I couldna say*

*How much how dear I love thee.*
*I see thee dancing o'er the green,*
*Thy waist sae gimp thy limbs sae clean,*
*Thy tempting lips, thy roguish een-*
*By Heav'n and Earth I love thee!*

From 'O Were I on Parnassus Hill' – written to Jean Armour.

Burns was a man of contrasts – as we all are; who on earth would like anyone, excluding myself, who is perfect? At the end of the day, though, Burns was a wordsmith at the top of his game, and a craftsman whose metre simply carries you along without you noticing. Read 'Tam o' Shanter', possibly Burns' most famous poem. It is a larger-than-life tale of a farmer, Tam (Tom), who, against his wife's advice, stays too long in the pub with his cronies and, galloping home between night and morning, comes upon witches and warlocks dancing, with the Devil playing the pipes, in Alloway's Auld Kirk. Tam is chased and escapes by riding over the Brig o' Doon (the Bridge of Doon) and the rushing water beneath, which witches are unable to cross – though Tam's trusty mare, Meg, loses her tail to Nannie, the witch (who wears a cutty-sark, a short nightdress). The piece is brilliant: exciting, at times hilarious and bawdy, it is also full of rich imagery and Burns' affection for legend. Moreover, the characters are based on people he knew and have become part of his story: clever!

I'm pretty sure I would have enjoyed the company of Robert Burns, especially over a few jars. It is possible we might have disagreed on politics, but I like to think we would have had pleasure in the debate. You can't help wondering what he would have achieved if he had lived longer.

## Places associated with Robert Burns
There is no shortage of shrines for the pilgrims of Burns, especially in Ayrshire and neighbouring Dumfries and

Galloway. There are also statues of him all over the world. According to The Scotsman, "excluding religious figures Burns has more statues around the world than any figure living or dead save for Christopher Columbus and Queen Victoria." You'll find one very imposing statue of Robert Burns in Victoria Embankment Gardens, not far from the Houses of Parliament in London.

The picturesque village of Alloway is home to the Robert Burns Birthplace Museum, as well as Burns' Cottage, where he was born and lived until he was 7, Alloway Old Kirk, the Brig o' Doon and the Burns Memorial Garden, where there is an enormous Burns Monument. Down the road from Alloway is the village of Kirkoswald, where you'll find the graves of Burns' grandparents and great-grandparents in the old kirkyard. Also buried there are Robert's teacher from his time at Kirkoswald School, as well as Tam o' Shanter (Douglas Graham) and Souter Johnnie (John Davidson) – another character from the poem. A 'souter' was a shoemaker – and Souter Johnnie's cottage, now housing local artwork, together with a small brewhouse (alas, no longer in use) in the garden, are also in the village and open to the public. (As a further attraction, inside the ruins of the old kirk is the font where Robert the Bruce was christened in 1274.) There's another museum in Dumfries in the house Burns shared with Jean. He is buried in St Michael's churchyard – and his favourite howff, the Globe Inn, is still there.

## Burns' Night

The first recorded Burns celebration was held just 5 years after his death, in July 1801. Burns Suppers can be incredibly serious at one extreme, or an orgy of food, alcohol and poetry at the other. Go for something in between and see how you get on. The essential ingredients are:

▪ Haggis and other traditional Scottish food;

- Whisky (wine and ale are acceptable too, but not as a substitutes – and, please note, it has to be whisky, not whiskey);
- Music and poetry celebrating Robbie Burns;
- A chairperson (usually, but not necessarily, the host/ess) and readers/performers from among the guests, appointed well in advance, to undertake the necessary constituent parts of the evening.

## A GUIDE TO YOUR BURNS' NIGHT

### *Piping in the guests.*
Or, if you don't have a piper, have someone play some traditional Scottish music – preferably live, but recorded will do nicely too.

### *The welcome*
The host/ess or chairperson makes sure everyone is welcomed and introduced.

### *The Selkirk Grace*
Burns is believed to have written this in the Selkirk Arms, Kirkcudbright:

*Some hae meat and canna eat,*
*And some wad eat that want it,*
*But we hae meat and we can eat,*
*And sae the Lord be thankit.*

### *Starter*
A traditional starter is cock-a-leekie soup, but something with Scottish smoked salmon often goes down well.

### *Piping in the haggis*
The haggis is announced with a piper (if you have one) or by some other splendid Scottish musical means. Stick the haggis

on your best silver platter (or nearest equivalent). Guests should be invited to stand as the haggis comes in and the opportunity should be taken to ensure that everyone's glass is full. On very formal occasions, there's a small procession of piper, cook/chef and someone to address the haggis.

### The address to a Haggis

*Fair fa' your honest, sonsie face,*
*Great chieftain o' the pudding-race!*
*Aboon them a' yet tak your place,*
*Painch, tripe, or thairm:*
*Weel are ye wordy o'a grace*
*As lang's my arm.*

There's more. At the appropriate moment… *His knife see rustic Labour dight*…the person giving the address dramatically cuts the length of the haggis with a very sharp knife, making sure the contents spill out…

*His knife see rustic Labour dight,*
*An' cut you up wi' ready sleight,*
*Trenching your gushing entrails bright,*
*Like ony ditch;*
*And then, O what a glorious sight, Warm-reekin', rich!*
*Toast: "to the haggis!"*

### Main course

Haggis, neeps and tatties. Haggis is either:
- A small furry creature living in remote parts of the Highlands, hunted remorselessly as a delicacy and eaten whenever possible;
- Minced offal (lamb and beef), with oatmeal, onions, suet and spices, cooked in a bag (traditionally, an animal's stomach).

Haggis is traditionally served with neeps (turnips, mashed)

and tatties (mashed potatoes). Some add mashed carrot too – and it's great!

### Dessert

Typical options include Tipsy Laird (an alcoholic trifle, often using sherry); Ecclefechan tart (a tart made with dried fruit and spices); clootie dumpling (a fruity suet pudding).

### To follow

A selection of Scottish cheeses, oatcakes and coffee.

### Entertainment

A guest should perform a Burns song or recite one of his poems at this point.

### The immortal memory

A well-researched, rehearsed, captivating discourse on the life and genius of Robert Burns, quoting from his works and concluding with the toast, "to the Immortal Memory of Robert Burns!"

### More entertainment

See above.

### Toast to the Lassies

Using suitable quotations from Burns' works, and ideally making appropriate reference to the ladies present, a speaker praises women. It's a broad brief, but should be amusing and always tasteful. "To the Lassies!"

### Even more entertainment

See above again.

### Reply to the Toast to the Lassies

This is the chance for a chosen lady, on behalf of all members of her sex present, to retaliate.

*Auld Lang Syne*
Everyone sings, even those unable to stand.

After that - it's up to you..!

   \* Sassenach is supposedly an abusive Scots' term for an Englishman; it is derived from the Gaelic for Saxon.

# 4
# VALENTINE'S DAY
## 14 February

 When you are old and grey, and full of sleep, shall I compare thee to a summer's day; or do you walk in beauty, like the night, down by the Sally Garden? Shall I count the ways I loved you, will they stop the clocks, cut off the telephone, leaving me palely loitering, all alone? Yet, I'll remember the first day, first hour, first moment, first time; and you will still be my Valentine.

Everyone knows that 14th February is Valentine's Day. Britain's (allegedly) most romantic day is for some the gladdest; for others, perhaps, the saddest. Don't bother to stifle your groan at the appalling rhyme – the day is renowned for them. The ditty below dates from 1784:

*The rose is red, the violet's blue,*
*The honey's sweet, and so are you.*

Oh dear.

Undeterred by asinine verse, you may even now be listening eagerly for the postman, in hopeful, delicious, anticipation of the arrival of a card, a note – something, anything – dropping onto the doormat from the one you love; anonymously, of course. And how about you? What will you do to prevent your Valentine's Day being a massacre? Surely not an impersonal email, text, or whatever electronic message; what are you thinking?! Apparently, some smooth Casanovas ask for dates by these, or similar, eye-contact avoiding means; is the Digital Age making us impersonal in affairs of the heart, cowards in love?

Valentine's Day is a special day, an opportunity to remind that particular person how much they are loved, and perhaps spend a little romantic time together. Maybe you want to let someone know how you feel, just in case they're unaware of it. Maybe you simply want to quietly remember someone. But, will you make someone's pulse race and send a card? Will you give or receive roses? Chocolates? Champagne? Plan a romantic dinner, or weekend away? It is common, apparently, to propose marriage on Valentine's Day. Some, I hear, risk getting the elbow if they don't demonstrate their undying affection in some appropriate manner on this Annual Day of Love. The owner of one card shop confided in me that she once had a customer chappie who was adamant that he wouldn't get his tea if he didn't buy his wife a Valentine's card; calamitous stuff! But this was in the north of England, where men can't make their own tea; allowances need to be made.

Bizarrely – and you may find this difficult to understand (as well as slightly unsavoury) – according one survey 4.5% of Brits buy a Valentine's gift for their pet dog. I'm trying to imagine what Fido would make of that; though I can imagine what a psychologist might say.

C'mon – take this seriously, will you?

## The business of Valentine's Day

You won't be surprised to learn that Valentine's Day is big business. Huge. The website statista.com says that the UK Valentine market is worth £855 million, whereas finder.com goes even further to an eye-watering £1.45 billion. Whatever – it is a great deal of money, and probably more than I will earn from this book. The popular purchases are food and drink, jewellery, flowers and clothing. We splash the cash on Valentine's Day cards, too, of course; nearly £46 million in 2018 according to the Greeting Card Association (and they should know). The GCA also maintains that most greetings cards overall are bought from high street shops, rather than online; so, hopefully, our card shops are unlikely to fold.

Most people – that's more than 50% - spend something on their beloved Valentine partners (presumably, this includes dogs, cats, iguanas, goldfish etc). Men spend more than women, Londoners more than any other part of the country and Millennials (those born between 1981 and 1996) are the highest spending age-group. Dogs don't spend much at all, apparently, wherever they live and however old they are.

### The origins and history of Valentine's Day

That's all very well; but how did Valentine's Day start?

We begin with *Lupercalia*, the feast of *Lupercus*, the Roman god of fertility. Of course we do. Lupercalia is a very ancient festival indeed, with obscure roots far beyond my ability to concentrate and with connections to the she-wolf who nursed Romulus and Remus, the very founders of Rome. Rituals included the sacrifice of a goat (or two) and a dog, whose hides would be cut into thongs which were then used to gently whip willing women. The whipping was carried out by scantily clad, or naked, chaps and was, as you would expect, intended to make the ladies fertile. I daresay strong drink was involved somewhere too. Lupercalia is also associated with Februa, the feast of purification, for which the month of February is named. It's not entirely clear to me whether Februa became Lupercalia, or the other way round. The point is that it occurred either on 15th February, or between 13th and 15th February – depending who you believe. And some think this might have been the origin of our Valentine's Day. I like to imagine that the animals – certainly the dogs – were given a nice Lupercalia Day gift before being dispatched, but they probably weren't; sorry.

Next into the murky mythical mix comes St Valentine himself. Or St Valentines, because there seem to have been at least two of the little loves. One tale that is repeated in varying versions is that our Valentine – or Valentinus - was a third century bishop in Rome who, in defiance of an imperial ban on soldiers marrying, conducted wedding ceremonies for young couples in secret, thus incurring the wrath of the authorities. Whilst imprisoned for his heinous crimes (presumably, performing weddings without a licence), Valentine fell in love with the blind daughter of his gaoler, Asterious, and restored her sight. In no account that I have seen is she given a name; she is, simply, the daughter of Asterious. Anyway, following this miracle, Asterious promptly converted to Christianity and instructed his entire household to follow his example. However, Emperor Claudius, having nothing better to do, and presumably fed up with Valentine's irritating monotheism when there were so many other nice gods to choose from, ordered that Valentine be beaten with clubs, stoned and then decapitated. Before his execution, which allegedly took place on 14th February, Valentine sent his poor, nameless, sweetheart a farewell note signed, "from your Valentine." The very first Valentine's Day message. He was buried on the Via Flaminia in Rome; though, like all the best saints, St Valentine's remains are scattered – in his case as far apart as Prague, Chelmno, Vienna and Glasgow. One of his skulls is in Rome's Santa Maria Basilica, whilst his body, or one very much like it, rests in Whitefriar Street Church, Dublin. His feast day – Valentine's Day - was announced as 14th February by the Pope in 495 AD. As well as being the patron saint of lovers, St Valentine is the patron saint of young people, epileptics, fainting, beekeepers and plague.

Almost 900 years pass until we next hear of Valentine's Day. Sometime in the late 14th century, Geoffrey Chaucer, the father of English literature, wrote a humorous poem exploring the idea of love called 'Parlement of Foules'. In the middle ages, people thought that birds mated in February:

*For this was on seynt Volantynys day*
*Whan euery foul comyth there to chese his make.*

Some believe this was the origin of St Valentine's Day being a day for lovers. It was certainly established in France as a day to celebrate romantic love by the 15th century. The Duke of Orleans, imprisoned in the Tower of London after the Battle of Agincourt in 1415, wrote a poem to his wife, which has the refrain:

*Je suis desja d'amour tanné*
*Ma tres doulce Valentinée*

I am already sick of love, my very gentle Valentine. Probably the oldest surviving Valentine's Day greeting in English was written by a young Norfolk woman, Margery Brews, to her cousin and fiancé, John Paston, in 1477. In it, she calls John, "my right well beloved Valentine" and says that she won't be in good health until she hears from him.

There are unsubstantiated claims all over the Internet that either Henry VII or VIII declared Valentine's Day a holiday in 1537. Well, it is unlikely to have been Henry VII, because he died in 1509. And it is probably an urban myth that Henry VIII did such a thing – though you never know with Henry, I suppose; he may have been sufficiently besotted with Jane Seymour in February 1537, before her untimely death later in the year. But Shakespeare certainly mentions Valentine's Day a couple of times, most famously in Hamlet when Ophelia sings:

*To-morrow is Saint Valentine's day,*
*All in the morning betime,*
*And I a maid at your window,*
*To be your Valentine.*

The 'roses are red, violets are blue' line also dates from the 16th century, from Sir Edmund Spenser's Faerie Queene:

*She bath'd with roses red, and violets blew,*
*And all the sweetest flowres, that in the forrest grew.*

Samuel Pepys, royal naval administrator, philanderer and bar, and sometime diarist, mentions Valentine often.

The first Valentine's cards appeared in the 18th century, initially hand-made and containing encouraging words, they were surreptitiously tied to door knockers or slipped under doors. Chaps whose affections, whilst absolutely genuine and honourable, were nevertheless inadequate to inspire soft, romantic, murmurings, could consult special prepared Valentine's writer pamphlets and select an appropriate verse with which to woo the object of their desires. ("Down, Fido!")

Eventually, printed cards became available. What is possibly the oldest printed Valentine's card in the world is held by York Castle Museum. It was published in 1797, in London, and includes this verse around the edge:

*Since on this ever Happy day,*
*All Nature's full of Love and Play*
*Yet harmless still if my design,*
*'Tis but to be your Valentine.*

The card was sent by a Catherine Mossday to a Mr Brown of Dover Place, Kent Road, London. Inside, Catherine wrote:

"Mr Brown,
As I have repeatedly requested you to come I think you must have some reason for not complying with my request, but as I have something particular to say to you I could wish you make it all agreeable to come on Sunday next without fail and in doing you will oblige your well-wisher.
Catherine Mossday".

Intriguing…you can't help wondering whether Mr Brown obliged Miss Mossday on Sunday. Mass-produced Valentine's Day cards appeared in the 19th century and, by the mid-1820s, an estimated 200,000 cards were in circulation around London. With the introduction of the uniform Penny Post in 1840, the number of cards doubled by the end of that decade and, according to the Museum of London – which has a collection of more than 1,700 Valentine's cards – doubled again by the 1860s. Valentine cards began to be exported to the USA, where they were promoted as a British thing. So much for our famous reserve.

As well as ornate, romantic, cards that were made with lace paper and decorated with images of flowers, birds and cupids, the Victorians produced some amusing, as well as some less elaborate, offensive cards. So-called 'vinegar', or 'mocking Valentines' were designed to tease – or hurt - perhaps lampooning a man's profession, character, or even a woman's appearance.

It is said that the Victorians considered it bad luck to sign a Valentine's Day card. Who knows; maybe young men were terrified of Victorian dads and young ladies didn't want to appear too forward. Or, maybe we're all inspired by that very first greeting, "from your Valentine".

# 5
# SHROVE TUESDAY
## February or March

Pancake Day, or Shrove Tuesday, is the day before Ash Wednesday, which is the start of Lent. The 40 days of Lent commemorate Christ's sacrifice and withdrawal in the desert and used to be a traditional time of fasting for Christians. These days, you're simply meant to give up something you like – a favourite food, for example (but not chocolate, obviously). So, 'shrove' is the past tense of the old verb 'shrive', meaning to hear confession. If you have been shriven, you've already done it and declared your sins before Lent.

It is called Pancake Day because it became traditional to eat pancakes then. The shrove-bell calling people to confession became known as 'the pancake bell'. The humble pancake is basically batter and uses up ingredients that people might have lying around – eggs, flour, fat and milk – so that they could fill themselves up before lean Lent. Pancakes have been eaten for centuries, apparently, at least as far back as the ancient Greeks and Romans. On their own, they can be fairly bland so it's usual to flavour them with something – lemon juice and caster sugar are common, but I reckon you could experiment a bit.

Here is a recipe I found in a cookbook from the 1920s (every home should have one):

INGREDIENTS
Milk - ½ pint (285 ml)
Plain flour - 8 ounces (226 g)
Eggs – 2
Oil – dessert spoon
Salt - pinch

METHOD

Mix all together and whisk well. Heat a little oil in a frying pan, pour in enough batter to cover the base of the pan thinly. When set, shake the pan and loosen the pancake, turn it over and cook the other side.

Please don't let me know how you get on.

It is traditional to toss the pancake to turn it. From there, it is easy to see how this could develop into a race – and pancake races are still held in parts of the UK, often with competitors wearing fancy dress. Aside from that, pancakes are still made by mums and dads for their children on Shrove Tuesday, without most people having much of a clue why.

Shrove Tuesday always falls 47 days before Easter Sunday, so the date varies from year to year sometime between early February and early March.

# 6
# ST DAVID'S DAY
## 1 March

 St David is the patron saint of Wales. The problem with saints' days is that most Britons do not believe in saints. However, they are regarded by many as occasions to celebrate national characteristics and cultures, and St David's Day on 1st March is no exception. Very little is known about David, Dafydd, or Dewi; he lived in the 5th/6th centuries and is the only patron saint of any British nation to be a native.

## Who was St David?

The story goes that David's mother, St Non, or Nonnita, was raped by Xantus, or Sanctus, Prince of Cereticu (Ceredigion), and the product of this violation was David. Non, who may have been a nun and the daughter of a chieftain, gave birth to her son on a clifftop during a wild storm. Today, the ruins of St Non's Chapel on the Pembrokeshire coast mark the spot. Generally, the year of David's birth is given as anywhere between 462 and 515 AD.

St David grew up to become a celebrated preacher and founder of monasteries and churches throughout Wales, southwest England and Brittany. Some say he founded Glastonbury Abbey. He is also reputed to have made a pilgrimage to Jerusalem. In the little green valley of the River Alun, an area known as Mynyw, David established the monastic centre that would come to bear his name, St Davids. His rule was austere: the monks wore animal skins, did not eat meat, drink beer, had no personal possessions and laboured hard – including ploughing the fields by hand - to sustain themselves as well as help feed the local poor. This lifestyle obviously did David no harm at all; he became a bishop and some say he lived to 100, dying on 1st March – which, by uncanny coincidence, is St David's Day. The year of his death is often given as 589AD, but you won't be surprised to hear that alternative dates are available. He was buried in the church that he founded, on the site of today's St David's Cathedral, where you will still find his shrine.

The leek has long been associated with Wales and St David. It is said that Welsh soldiers wore leeks in their helmets to distinguish themselves from their Anglo-Saxon enemies in battle – indeed some say that David ordered this, though it is hard to picture this highly spiritual man indulging in anything as vulgar as war.

In the last sermon he gave, he told his followers to, "Be joyful, keep the faith, and do the little things that you have heard and seen me do." The phrase *'Gwnewch y pethau bychain mewn bywyd'* - 'Do the little things in life' - is still a well-known Welsh saying.

## Stories about St David

St David's monastic settlement gained reputation as a place of holiness and learning. The saint's resting place became a place of pilgrimage and St Davids went on to become the wealthiest diocese in medieval Wales. The status of St Davids was such that even the 9th century King of the West Saxons, Alfred the Great, sought help from it; the Welsh monk Asser was dispatched eastward to assist in the restoration of spiritual and intellectual life in the wake of the devastation caused by warfare with the Danes. Mind you, Alfred, ever the pragmatist, may have been motivated by the desire to unite Celt and Saxon against the common foe. St Davids was always a handy location too, for visitors dropping by en route to or from Ireland. But this, as well as the magnet of its prosperity, could be a drawback; because Viking raiders attacked a dozen times in the 10th and 11th centuries, twice killing the bishop (being killed once must have been bad enough).

One story told about David concerns his teacher, Paulinus. Paulinus was an elderly man and going blind. David gently touched the old man's eyes, restoring his sight.

St David's best-known miracle, however, took place in the village of Llanddewi Brefi, at the synod held there. David was addressing the crowd and, so that all could see and hear him, the ground he was standing on rose up to form a hill. This was necessary because, of course, there are so few hills in Wales. And then a white dove was seen to settle on the saint's shoulder; the white dove remains one of David's emblems.

### Why is David the patron saint of Wales?

The 5th and 6th centuries have been called the 'Age of the Saints' in Wales and Welsh tradition features many evangelising figures, all journeying the seaways between Brittany, Cornwall, Wales and Ireland, spreading the Word. Somehow, David emerged from this as the pre-eminent figure. He was canonised by Pope Callistus II in the 12th century, is the only Welsh saint to be canonised by the Roman Catholic church and St David's Day has been a national festival for centuries.

### How important is St David today?

St David has his own flag – a yellow cross on a black background – but, unlike the flags of St George, St Andrew and St Patrick, it is not incorporated into the Union Flag. Neither is the national flag of Wales – the red dragon on the white and green background. Both flags only really date from the 20th century, though the red dragon, *Y Ddraig Goch*, is an ancient symbol, and green and white were the colours of the Tudors, whose origins were Welsh.

St David's Day is widely celebrated as a national day in Wales, when it is traditional to wear the national emblems of a leek or a daffodil. It is not yet a public holiday, despite support for this from the National Assembly for Wales. Parades take place in Cardiff, and other places (possibly including villages like Llareggub), lessons are often put aside in schools, traditional costumes worn, eisteddfods held and leek broth consumed. It is a salutation to Welshness, which includes the language (still the first language of many in Wales), singing and the obsession with rugby - in which the national team consistently punches above its weight. The daffodil, incidentally, was encouraged as a Welsh emblem by the politician David Lloyd George (Prime Minister from 1916-1922), but no one seems sure why. Whilst mentioning famous Welshfolk, we shouldn't forget (in no particular order), Bonnie Tyler, Catherine-Zeta Jones, Anthony Hopkins, Richard Burton, Tom Jones, Aneurin Bevan, Dylan Thomas, Shirley Bassey, Gareth Edwards, JPR Williams and Ryan Giggs (probably).

But St David is seen by some as the ultimate Welshman. Indeed, apparently, the nickname 'Taffy' is derived from 'Dafydd', the Welsh for David. Bet you're really glad you bought this book now.

# 7

# ST PATRICK'S DAY
## 17 March

 St Patrick is the patron saint of Ireland. So why, you may reasonably ask, does he feature in a book about Britain? Well, one good reason is that Patrick, unlike the patron saints of England and Scotland, was actually British. Another reason is that there are an awful lot of people in Britain of Irish descent – and of course Northern Ireland is part of the United Kingdom. Finally, it could be argued that St Patrick's Day is celebrated more widely in Britain than the feast days of the patron saints of England, Scotland, or Wales. Or maybe it's just that some people need an excuse to go to the pub.

**Who was St Patrick?**
Patrick is believed to have been a real person, although (inevitably) facts are few. Despite confident claims to the contrary, we do not know exactly when or where Patrick was born, lived, or died. We do have two works which are generally agreed to have been written by him, the *Confessio* (Confession) and the *Epistola* (Letter to Coroticus), though the copies in existence were produced long after Patrick had gone to meet his maker. In his Confession, he writes:

> "My name is Patrick. I am a sinner, a simple country person, and the least of all believers. I am looked down upon by many. My father was Calpornius. He was a deacon; his father was Potitus, a priest, who lived at Bannavem Taburniae."

Bannavem Taburniae has not been positively identified. Patrick was born, sometime in the 5th century, most likely somewhere on the west coast of Britain: perhaps Wales, perhaps Scotland, perhaps Cumbria – though none of those places were known by those names at the time, of course. This was sub-Roman Britain, the period after Roman rule had ended and long before countries like England, Scotland and Wales were twinkles in anybody's eye. So, Patrick might be described as Romano-British, and possibly came from a reasonably well-off background. Actually, he may originally have had another name - Maewyn Succat, only becoming Patricius later. But let's stick with Patrick. When he was 16-ish, he was captured by Irish raiders, taken across the sea to their homeland and enslaved. For six years, the young man worked as a herdsman, traditionally on Slemish, a volcanic plug in County Antrim, and it was during that time that he found Christianity. One night, he had a dream that a ship was waiting to take him home, so he escaped to the coast, 200 miles away (allegedly), and talked himself a passage back to Britain.

After several adventures, he was reunited with his loving family. He is said to have been visited by an angel in a dream, who told him that he should return to Ireland to spread God's word. It is possible he travelled to Gaul to train as a priest. But, eventually, he did go back to Ireland where, legend has it, he converted everyone to Christianity. This sounds a trifle exaggerated, even allowing for a smaller population in those far-off days, and it's probable that Christianity had already arrived in Ireland before Patrick got there anyway. Nonetheless, he does seem to have been extremely successful at winning folk over – and, let's face it, converting pagan, illiterate, and presumably sometimes sceptical, even antagonistic, people cannot have been easy. Various accounts suggest he was often in danger – and that sounds likely. Patrick, like other early evangelists, must have been an extraordinary man.

## Stories about St Patrick

As with other saints, Patrick has his share of associated legends and myths, including accounts of raising the dead and duelling with druids. The two most famous tales, however, are the ones about snakes and the shamrock. The reason there are no snakes in Ireland, 'tis said, is that Patrick drove them all into the sea. The most popular St Patrick tradition, however, is that he used the shamrock, a trefoil plant, to explain the Holy Trinity – three distinct entities in one: God the Father, God the Son, God the Holy Ghost. There's a bit of confusion over what, exactly, a shamrock is – or was. Some say it's clover, others say it's wood sorrel; but the Irish *seamróg* apparently means 'small clover'. Whatever the shamrock is, to this day it is the national plant of Ireland. Just make sure it has three leaves, not four.

Sadly, experts believe that the shamrock story only dates from the 17th century. Worse, it wasn't warm enough for snakes to reach Ireland until after melting glaciers turned the sea into an impassable barrier, by which time it was too late. There is just one native reptile in Ireland, the common lizard, so there were never any snakes for Patrick to banish. However, snakes can be seen as symbols for serpents; therefore Patrick, by spreading Christianity, was banishing evil. Ergo, the snake story is probably allegorical.

Perhaps the best story about Patrick, though, has never been told. Several articles suggest Patrick harboured a guilty secret. In his Confessio, he wrote that some of his superiors brought up an embarrassing matter that he had confessed to previously, "some things I had done one day – rather, in one hour – when I was young, before I overcame my weakness. I don't know – God knows – whether I was then fifteen years old at the time, and I did not then believe in the living God, not even when I was a child." I think we'll leave the mind boggling at what he may have got up to as a teenager. But, whatever it was, he seems to have regarded his work in Ireland as some kind of penance for his sins.

## Why is Patrick the patron saint of Ireland?

Patrick's association with Ireland is undeniable. His crowning achievement was spreading Christianity in Ireland as well as being partly responsible (albeit indirectly) for its introduction by St Columba to the Picts in Scotland - and thence to the Anglo-Saxons in northern England. Accordingly, Patrick is known as the 'Apostle of Ireland' and is venerated alongside Columba and Brigid of Kildare. Patrick was never formally canonised, however. His feast day, 17th March, is believed to have been the date of his death and placed firmly into the church calendar due to the influence of Waterford-born Franciscan monk and scholar, Luke Wadding (1588-1657).

Some say that Patrick died at Saul, where he built his first church, near Downpatrick – where he is reputedly buried in the churchyard of Down Cathedral.

## How important is St Patrick today?

St Patrick's flag, the red saltire on a white background, is relatively recent and dates from the 18th century. It is one of the three elements that make up the Union Flag (Union Jack), the other two being the crosses of St George and St Andrew.

Although saints' days are traditionally religious occasions that commemorate the appropriate individual and their works, St Patrick's Day has become a festival of all things Irish and is celebrated all over the world, often with parades – notably where there are large communities that have Irish origins – such as the USA, where parades began in Boston and New York in the 18th century. In modern Britain, notable parades take place in London, Birmingham, Liverpool, Manchester and Glasgow. The colour green predominates, people dress as kitsch leprechauns, there is traditional music, much dancing, shamrocks are everywhere and a great deal of Guinness is consumed.

Astonishingly, a poll in 2019 listed the vocalist, Bono, as

the most famous Irish person ever. Other candidates included (in no particular order) also-rans like Oscar Wilde, WB Yeats and James Joyce; then we shouldn't forget Liam Neeson, Graham Norton, Pierce Brosnan, Michael Collins, Shane MacGowan, Enya and the Corrs.

# 8
# **EASTER**
## March or April

 It should be simple enough to write a bit about Easter, I thought. After all, it is the most important festival in the Christian calendar, and a good deal of Britain's heritage, at least for the last fourteen centuries or more, has been informed by a Christian tradition. So we should be sure of our ground, shouldn't we? Of course, everyone knows that a touch of paganism creeps into our rituals here and there too, adding a little juice and shedding a dim light on some of our even older customs.

It is asking for trouble when you say things like, 'everyone knows'.

### A bit about Easter

Let's start with the easier bit, the Easter story. It is a powerful tale, from Jesus's arrival in Jerusalem on Palm Sunday, through to the Last Supper (Maundy Thursday), arrest, trial and the awful suffering of the crucifixion on Good Friday. Jesus's body is placed in a guarded cave tomb, the entrance to which is covered with an enormous rock. But, by Sunday, the rock had been mysteriously moved and the body had vanished. The authorities believed it had been stolen. But the disciples believed Jesus had been resurrected. This, of course, is at the heart of Christianity. The crucifixion and resurrection mobilised an entire religion. Life triumphs over death, there is a new beginning, a re-birth.

Even a contented cynic like me can respect the Easter story, and the faith behind it; nor would most people dispute that Easter is anything other than a Christian celebration. Though I'm sure the lost scrolls of Horus, the saga of the great pink pixie and other bits of faux twaddle have plenty of alternatives to offer, none of them has made much difference to Britain.

But why is Easter called Easter in Britain, and in other English-speaking places?

Well, many people believe there is some kind of association with an ancient deity, *Eostre*, or *Ostara*, a Germanic goddess of dawn. You regularly come across things like the following, which is from that font of often useless and occasionally dodgy knowledge, 'The Reader's Digest Book of Strange Stories, Amazing Facts':

"Eostre is the Goddess of Dawn and her festival is held around the vernal equinox, the date when day and night are of equal length."

That's pretty definite – as are many other references you come across. The problem is that it assumes a great deal, because Eostre is about as elusive as the real Easter bunny. In fact, the only historical reference to Eostre was made by our old chum Bede in *De ratione temporum*, 'On the reckoning of Time', written in 725AD. In this, talking of the names by which the English (Anglo-Saxons) knew the months of the year, Bede says of April:

"Eosturmonath has a name which is now translated 'Paschal month', and which was once called after a goddess of theirs named Eostre, in whose honour feasts were celebrated in that month. Now they designate that Paschal season by her name, calling the joys of the new rite by the time-honoured name of the old observance."

Bede does not elaborate and, other than that single reference, there is apparently no other historic evidence for the existence of this goddess. No statues, no amulets, no memorials, fridge magnets – nothing. We hear plenty about other gods - Tiw, Woden, Thunor and Frig (*Tiwesdaeg, Wodensdaeg, Thunresdaeg, Frigedaeg*); but nothing about Eostre. Then there's the etymology of eostre in its various forms; it is almost certainly old German, possibly derived from the word for east or sunrise. So, was Bede right? He often wasn't. But, on the balance of probability, he would be unlikely to make it up. So did the Anglo-Saxons worship a great goddess of the sunrise, a good witch of the east, equivalent to the Roman goddess of dawn, Aurora, or the Greek, Eos? It is quite possible, even probable, that they did, even if only at a local level. The trouble is, we simply don't know.

Anyway, the fact is that, for some unknown reason, the biggest event in the Christian calendar appears to have a non-Christian name in the English-speaking world. Was this another example of the early church making use of existing custom and practice? There is an awful lot about this on the Internet, some of it interesting, some of it sharing similar ground with the Hobbit.

You might be interested to hear that another old chum, the Rev E Cobham Brewer, in his wonderful 'Dictionary of Phrase & Fable' (1894 edition), refers to April – *Ostermonath* – as the month of the ost (east) wind. He also says that it was formerly a common belief that the sun danced on Easter Day. Everyone knows that.

## The timing of Easter

"When is Easter this year?" I'm very glad that you asked. It is believed that Christ celebrated the Last Supper on the first day of the Jewish celebration of Passover (Pesach in Hebrew), which dates back to about 1300BC and commemorates the liberation of the Children of Israel, when Moses led them out of Egypt. We still use the adjective 'paschal', derived from the Latin (via Greek and Hebrew) for Passover, to refer to Easter. Because of this, the dates of

Easter and Passover – which are both movable feasts - often coincide. The First Council of Nicaea in 325AD, the first official meeting of church authorities, determined that Easter should be the first Sunday following the paschal full moon, which is the full moon that falls on or after the vernal (spring) equinox. Differences in calendars mean that Western Christians celebrate Easter on different dates to some of their Eastern Orthodox brethren. There are those who would like a fixed date, but after two thousand years there's obviously no urgency to agree one.

In Britain, the timing of Easter could have been different. Pop into the famous Yorkshire seaside town of Whitby, known for its fish 'n' chips, jet jewellery and associations with Captain Cook and Dracula, but less well-known as the place where the timing of Britain's Easter holiday was decided. Christianity petered out in much of Britain after the end of Roman rule, but was carried on in the 5th and 6th centuries in Celtic communities in western parts of the island, and then Ireland. The religion eventually spread, via Strathclyde in what is now southern Scotland, into Northumbria and the Anglo-Saxon kingdoms to the south. St Ninian is alleged to have founded a community at Whithorn in c397AD, St Columba set up a monastery on Iona in 563AD and a monastery was established on the island of Lindisfarne sometime around 634AD. Coming the other way, from the south, another brand of Christianity had been busy since 597AD, when St Augustine landed in Kent - on an official Papal Mission from Rome to convert the heathen Angles (English).

Now, there were great differences in ritual and organisation between the Roman and Celtic versions of Christianity. The monks even had different hairstyles – the Roman tonsure was the relatively familiar shaved round patch on the top of the head, whereas the Celtic tonsure ran from ear to ear at the front, leaving the hair long at the back. Rather more fundamentally, however, the two sects disagreed over how to calculate the date of Easter. I don't begin to understand the detail of this, which I personally find marginally less interesting than a block of concrete. All we really need to know is that the Celtic Christians used one formula and the Roman Catholics another. The King of Northumbria, Osuiu (or Oswy) was a committed Christian of the Celtic tradition. His wife Eanfled, however, had been brought up in Kent and followed the Roman way. This meant that the pair were in danger of celebrating Easter twice – imagine all that chocolate! Clearly, something had to be done. And Whitby was the place to do it, because here was Northumbria's principle church and minster, founded in 657AD by a remarkable lady, Hild, of the Celt party. So, the two sides, the Celtic and Roman, convened a synod at Whitby in 663 or 664 to debate the issues. Bishop Colman of Lindisfarne spoke for the Celts. The Roman case was then put by the Abbot of Ripon, Wilfred (later St Wilfred), who concluded by saying that the Roman Church received its authority from St Peter, holder of the keys to the Kingdom of Heaven. The Celts had no answer to that and Oswy (or Osuiu) found the argument pretty convincing, observing that if he did not obey the commands of the guardian of the gates of heaven, he might have some difficulty getting in when his time came. Ultimately, the Synod of Whitby determined which brand of Christianity ruled, not just when Easter would fall. And so, it came to pass that the Roman Church gained ascendancy over all others in the land, an authority that lasted some 900 years until the English Reformation in the 16th century.

### What about Easter eggs?

Eggs have long been a symbol of the universe, creation, life, fertility, rebirth and springtime, occurring in many ancient cultures – Persian, Egyptian, Jewish, Roman and Hindu, for example. In Christianity, the egg often represents the rebirth of man. There is also an association between eggs and Mary

Magdalene. One story says she took eggs to the tomb of Jesus, to share with the other women mourners there, but that when she met the risen Christ at the empty tomb, the eggs turned blood red. Colouring eggs red is, apparently, a Christian tradition. You probably won't find any of that in the Bible, though.

In Britain, it is thought that the tradition of Easter eggs developed in the Middle Ages because eggs were a ready source of food after Lent. Decorating eggs seems to have been a practice in several countries, particularly in the east, for many centuries. Several countries also have a custom of egg rolling, which some say originated with farmers hoping for fertile crops, and others say is symbolic of the stone rolling away from Jesus' tomb. In Britain, egg-rolling goes back centuries and is known as pace-egging – from Pasch – or Passover. It is apparently particularly popular in the north and is very big in Preston. In the 19th century, the custom was exported to the USA – where it is now part of the White House calendar – a timeless tradition since 1878…

In modern Britain, supermarket shelves groan under the weight of chocolate eggs. I spotted one in our local store, large and beautifully wrapped, going for more pounds than a decent bottle of single malt; what kind of idiot pays that much for a chocolate egg?! Then I found that Harrods was selling a Columbian milk chocolate egg for even more – but I guess that Columbian milk is special, and has to come a long way. From what I can make out, chocolate Easter eggs originated in France and Germany, but were first mass-produced by Cadbury in 1875; they were hollow and filled with sugared almonds. My personal favourites used to be small, caramel-filled eggs; they were about two inches long and came in a pack of about 8. Yum.

### And the Easter bunny?
Rabbits are not native to Britain – and neither is the Easter bunny. Mind you, some people think that the Easter bunny

was really a hare, and the hare does have a history in these islands, being regarded as both unlucky and lucky since the Middle Ages. It is suggested that witches readily turn into hares, though I've never witnessed that myself. Julius Caesar said the Celts of Britain deemed the hare to be sacred. These days, some folk will even tell you that the hare is a symbol of the goddess Eostre – you know, the one we don't know anything about. Be that as it may, the origins of the Paschal Bunny seem to depend on whether you subscribe to an egg-laying rabbit tradition (yes, really), an association with the Virgin Mary (which I don't even begin to understand), the obvious connection with fertility, birth etc (see 'bonking like bunnies') – or any combination thereof. I think you will search in vain for references to the Easter Bunny in the Bible. However, the arrival of this, frankly weird, beast on these shores, it seems, can be blamed on German or Dutch Lutherans, who took the idea of the *Osterhase*, the Easter rabbit (or hare) with them to the United States in the 18th century, from which it was exported back across the Atlantic, ostenwards as it were, to Britain. The Easter bunny allegedly distributes coloured eggs to children who have been good, a general notion which has a certain similarity with another time of year – just a different costume.

Naturally, like eggs, the Easter bunny is available in chocolate form. Harrods will sell you a Belgian one for a modest amount, though it's called Godiva which suggests it might not be modest at all. In fact, it is possible to obtain a wide variety of chocolate creatures at Easter, including (obviously) chicks and lambs. More mystifying are chocolate unicorns, cows, pigs, caterpillars, gruffalos and, suggesting that Easter is actually far older than the church thinks it is, chocolate dinosaurs.

**Hot cross buns**
For many of us, the hot cross bun is an Easter treat – though, sadly, they are now available most of the year round. They

don't have to be hot, but, arguably, they do need to be cut open and spread with butter. In Britain, a bun is kind of small, sweet loaf; hot cross buns traditionally contain raisins, mixed spices, candied peel and have a cross on top made of almond paste or shortcrust pastry. They were regarded as a post-Lent treat and traditionally eaten on Good Friday. An old rhyme, dating from the 18th century or earlier, will be familiar to many:

*Hot cross buns!*
*Hot cross buns!*
*One a penny, two a penny,*
*Hot cross buns!*

So, what is the origin of the hot cross bun? Well, like most of our Easter customs, it's a little hard to pin down, but the earliest reference seems to be as recent as 1733. The cross is obviously cited by the church as evidence of a Christian background. Thomas Dudley Fosbroke in 'British Monachism: or Manners and Customs of the Monks and Nuns of England' says that the buns were made of the dough kneaded for the host and were marked with the cross accordingly. That most reliable source, the Reader's Digest, says that women used to bake little 'magic' wheat cakes all over Europe around Easter. Brewer quotes Fosbroke and also goes on to say:

"The round bun represents the full moon and the cross represents the four quarters of the moon. They were made in honour of Diana by the ancient Roman priests, somewhere about the vernal equinox. Phoenicians, Carthaginians, Egyptians, Greeks and Romans worshipped the moon."

Various sources claim that two carbonised loaves marked with a cross were found in the ruins of Herculaneum, buried by the same eruption of Vesuvius that froze Pompeii in time in 79AD. Oh – and guess what? Pagan Saxons baked breads slashed with crosses to honour Eostre, goddess of spring and fertility; of course they did.

These days, they come in a bewildering variety of flavours, including chocolate (of course) and chilli (why?). The best news is that hot cross buns are meant to be lucky and are able to be kept for twelve months without turning mouldy. Yeah, right.

Ancient Easter joke: What do you get if you pour boiling water down a rabbit hole? Answer – a hot, cross, bunny.

## And, finally, Simnel cake

One Easter, many years ago, my mother announced we were going to have a Simnel cake. Despite this delicacy never appearing on any previous occasion, we were informed that this was a well-known Easter tradition and, after a duly dramatic baking session, the cake was produced with something of a flourish. And I haven't had it since. The reason I mention it now is because no one has suggested that Eostre baked one.

Simnel cake is meant to be a light fruit cake with a marzipan layer in the middle, a marzipan layer on top, and decorated with eleven marzipan balls, or eggs, representing Jesus's disciples minus Judas the traitor. It is then grilled for a short while and can, additionally, be decorated with flowers.

Its origins are unexpectedly obscure (please note, this book uses irony), but it seems to have once been associated with Mothering Sunday, the fourth Sunday of Lent. Some believe the name is derived from the Latin *simila*, referring to a very fine flour made from wheat. Other theories include the myth that the cake was created by Lambert Simnel, pretender to the English throne at the time of Henry VII, who was put to work in the royal kitchens – though Simnel cakes were known before that, apparently. The story I really like is that Simnel cake was invented by two people, Simon and Nell.

Oddly enough, Brewer says that Simnel cakes are rich cakes eaten in Lancashire in mid-Lent, and are of German origin.

Simnel cake is said to be quite difficult to make – which is why you'll find a recipe on the next page.

## RECIPE FOR GOOD SIMNEL CAKE

From the Richmond Cookery Book by Miss Lillie Richmond, published in 1897.

INGREDIENTS

| | |
|---|---|
| ½ lb sultanas | ¼ lb candied peel |
| 6 ozs castor sugar | ½ pint milk, lukewarm |
| 1 lb currants | ½ oz yeast |
| ½ nutmeg | 4 egg yolks |
| 1 teaspoonful spiced cinnamon | ¼ lb butter |
| ½ lb flour | |

METHOD

Rub the butter into the flour, add all the dry ingredients, mix well together. Cream the yeast, add to it the milk and yolks, make a well in the centre of the cake, and pour in the milk etc, mix into a soft paste, set to rise in a warm place for two hours.

Line a good sized round tin with thick paper, pour in half of the cake mixture, place a layer of almond paste in the centre, pour in remainder of cake mixture, bake two hours in a moderate oven.

---

## ALMOND PASTE FOR SIMNEL CAKE

INGREDIENTS

| | |
|---|---|
| ½ lb ground almonds | 2 eggs |
| ½ lb castor sugar | Flavouring essence |

METHOD

Put the sugar and almonds into a basin, add the essence, mix well, then make into a stiff paste with the yolks and white of one egg.

Author's note: I have no idea if this recipe is, actually, 'good'. The idea for the almond paste is that there's an additional, decorative, layer on top of the finished cake – whether the above quantities are sufficient is unknown. If there's enough mixture, use it to make balls or other shapes to go round the edge. I'm also advised that it's a good idea to brush the top of the cake with apricot jam before adding the almond paste topping. And an alternative to almond paste is marzipan. Oh – and an alternative recipe for almond paste will be found on page 114 after the A-Z of Christmas.

# 9
# ST GEORGE'S DAY
## 23 April

 St George is the patron saint of England. Curiously enough, 23rd April is also the day that William Shakespeare died (and it might even have been the day he was born). It was Shakespeare who put the words "Cry 'God for Harry! England and Saint George' " into the mouth of his King Henry V.

George killed the dragon. Most people know this; there are images and statues of it all over the world. George is usually associated with attributes like bravery, gallantry and honour – characteristics that the English may like to aspire to, but which are possibly not uniquely English. Worse, England has to share George with several other places, including Aragon, Catalonia, Georgia (the country, not the US state), Malta and Gozo, Portugal and Romania. George is the patron saint of Scouts, too, and is also said to help sufferers of syphilis. (Who decides these things?!) George's flag, a red cross on a white background, is the national flag of England, incorporated into the flag of the United Kingdom, the Union Flag, or Union Jack, which in turn is included in the flags of a score or so other nations and territories, including Australia, New Zealand and Hawaii. Further, the cross of St George is featured on the White Ensign flown by the Royal Navy, as well as on variants used by other navies around the world.

So, George is a global presence. There is a website, purporting to offer information about Britain, which claims that St George's Day is a favourite holiday. This will make many native Brits inwardly raise an eyebrow, because St George's Day is not a holiday (or it wasn't the last time I looked) and is not widely celebrated, not even in England. It is certainly celebrated in places, but most English people don't even notice it; on the other hand, many are happy to go out and get bladdered on St Patrick's Day, 17th March, ostensibly rejoicing the patron saint of a foreign country (albeit a jolly nice neighbour). In fairness, I suspect drinking to St Patrick is more about having a few beers, rather than particularly supporting the Emerald Isle, or anything else remotely subversive. All of this opens up a potentially adversarial, but interesting, debate about nationalism (there, I've used the 'n' word), patriotism, tribalism and the relevance or danger of these things in a modern world. But let's find out a bit about St George.

## Who was St George?

It is generally agreed that George existed and that we don't know much about him. There are various accounts of his life, including one that he was a mid-4th century Bishop of Alexandria, but the most common belief is that he was a Roman soldier. What follows is an attempt to blend the various popular legends in circulation. George was born to Christian parents, Gerontius and Polychronia, sometime around 275–285AD, somewhere in what is now modern Turkey – possibly in the Anatolian province of Cappadocia. Some sources suggest that his mother came from the Palestinian town of Lydda (now Lod in Israel) and that Gerontius had a successful career in the Roman army. George too joined the army, rising to the rank of Military Tribune (apparently equivalent to Colonel) and serving in Nicomedia (modern Izmit in Turkey), which the Emperor Diocletian (245–313AD) had made his eastern capital. Early in the 300s, Diocletian, hitherto fairly easy-going about different beliefs, was persuaded that Christian soldiers on parade were offending the gods by making the sign of the cross, and ordered that they should be expelled from the army unless they sacrificed in the traditional Roman way.

The story goes that George strongly objected to this and ignored various warnings to stop making such a fuss about it. When it reached the point where George's challenge to Imperial authority could no longer be tolerated, he was hideously tortured and, when he refused to deny his faith, he was decapitated on 23rd April 303AD. George was canonised by Pope Gelasius in 494AD.

**The story of George and the Dragon**
The legend of George and the Dragon may be based on a story far older than the legendary George himself. Nor did George have a monopoly in the dragon-slaying department; St Michael, the Anglo-Saxon hero Beowulf and the German hero Siegfried, among others, each had a certain way with unruly serpents. Dragon stories crop up all over the place. They often represent the triumph of good over evil; in Christianity, the dragon is sometimes seen as a metaphor for Satan. The dragon may have had particular significance to ancient Britons, however – and of course the red dragon is a symbol for Wales and features on the Welsh national flag.

You won't be surprised to learn that there are many versions of the George v Dragon tale, or that they involve different versions of George – including one whose home town was Coventry, in the English Midlands. However...

Once upon a time, there was a town in Libya called Silene where, next to a stagnant lake, lived a hungry dragon. The dragon was covered with hard green scales that could not be pierced by sword or spear, and had breath so foul it would clear a convention of sewage-workers. To keep the dragon fed, the townsfolk brought it two sheep each night. Eventually, they ran out of sheep and (obviously) had to resort to virgins, who were chosen by lot. All went swimmingly with this new arrangement until, one day, the king's daughter, Sabra, was selected. The king offered substantial bribes to release his daughter from her predicament but the villagers, who had by this time sacrificed many of their own children to the psychopathic insatiable reptile, were having none of it. So, at dinner-time, Sabra was duly led to the appointed place, tied to a stake, and left to her fate. Just when things were looking desperate, George came riding by and, seeing the weeping girl, naturally asked her what was up. Sabra explained, but urged George to ride on before the dragon appeared and ate him too. But our George was made of sterner stuff. Ignoring the water streaming from his eyes as a consequence of the creature's halitosis, he thrust his spear, called Ascalon, into the beast's mouth and killed him. The king was so chuffed, he told all his subjects to become Christians and built a whopping big church. George and Sabra married, retired (to Coventry?) and lived happily ever after. In some versions of the story, George promises to slay the dragon only on condition that the townsfolk convert to Christianity – but that seems a little small-minded, don't you think?

## Why is St George the patron saint of England?

You won't be surprised to hear that this is not an easy question to answer. Nor are the specifics behind George's rise to stardom clear. The fact that George was not English, never even popped in for a cuppa and had no known association with England whatsoever, seems to have been no hindrance to him being adopted as the nation's official saint; apparently, he merely needed to embody the appropriate characteristics, reflecting what were deemed to be English virtues. Deep-down, we'd all like to rescue damsels in distress.

Though there are early references to St George in England – including one in the 9th century will of Alfred the Great to the church of Fordington, Dorset, thought to be the first church in England dedicated to St George – the cult of St George (if it can be called that) came later. It is thought to have taken off when returning crusaders brought his story, popular with the Eastern Orthodox Church, back from the

Holy Land. It was claimed that visions of St George inspired men into battle - though their ultimate loyalty would have been to a feudal lord rather than to any then meaningless notion of 'nation'. Earlier saints said to have had significance for the English include St Edmund, martyred king of East Anglia, and Edward the Confessor – though what meaning these men would have had for Normans it is hard to say.

The red cross on a white background is not, of course, unique to St George; it was used by, amongst others, crusaders and the Knights Templar.

It seems that it was King Edward III (reigned 1327 – 1377) who put George at the centre of England, in c1348, by founding the College of St George at Windsor and associating it with the elite Order of the Garter. Even now, this is the highest order of chivalry and the third most prestigious honour (after the Victoria and George Crosses) in England and the United Kingdom. The arms of the order feature the cross of St George, surrounded by the gold and blue garter containing the motto *honi soit qui mal y pense* (shame on him who thinks evil of it). The badge shows George slaying the dragon.

Henry V, the first English king since Anglo-Saxon times to use English in his official letters, is said to have invoked St George at the Battle of Agincourt in 1415. Apparently, by Tudor times, the flag of St George was being flown from the monarch's ships.

### How important is St George today?

These days, apart from being occasionally hijacked by nationalist thugs (a common fate of national flags), the Cross of St George mainly flutters from church steeples, makes outings at football matches, and even some elections, but generally keeps a fairly low profile. Quite frankly, waving it around too much is viewed as being, at best, eccentric. It's not that the English aren't proud of who they are; it's simply that they're not sure what that means.

Of course, there are those who would like St George's Day to be a holiday in England, as St Andrew's Day is in Scotland. Among those are probably members of the Royal Society of St George, founded surprisingly recently, in 1894, "with the noble object of promoting 'Englishness' and the English way of life". This begs at least one question – what on earth is the nature of Englishness? It's a huge question, and one that of course any nation could ask of itself, but hard to answer in the context of a long British heritage and a United Kingdom. The English do not even have a national dress (unless it's something with clogs, handkerchiefs and bells) and probably have a less obvious sense of national identity than the Scots, Welsh or Irish. A debate on the subject included much uncertainty and nostalgia, plus the helpful suggestions of 'queues' and 'bowler-hats'. Here are a few more ideas: Agatha Christie, Jane Austen, Ale, BBC accents, The Beatles, Carols from King's, Cricket, Curry, Dark satanic mills, Charles Dickens, Drinking too much, Elgar, Elizabeth I, Fish and chips, Gardening, Hypocrisy, Lazy linguists, Mindless hooligans, Monty Python, Morris dancing, Net curtains, Isaac Newton, George Orwell, Pink Floyd, Politeness, The Reformation, Rupert Brooke, Satire, Shakespeare, stiff upper lip, White Cliffs of Dover, Wilfred Owen, Winnie the Pooh ...

# 10
# HALLOWEEN
## 31 October

 Your local supermarket resembles the props department for 'Night of the Living Dead'. There are plastic skulls, axes, hairy hands, spiders, broomsticks, masks more gruesome than many of the lost souls at the local shopping centre, and more besides. On one occasion I spotted a plastic fish skeleton – the relevance of which was lost on me. Pumpkins are everywhere – they only seem to hatch in Britain in October – and the colours orange and black predominate. Superficially, it's all quite light-hearted – I spotted some nice, girly, pink skeletons and was sorely tempted to buy a sparkly new, hopefully supercharged, broomstick for one of the more troublesome neighbours.

But, notwithstanding the rather attractive witch pictured in the costume display, some of this Halloween stuff is actually quite unpleasant. Before you say, "Yes, it's meant to be", pictures of small children made up to realistically resemble candidates for a post-mortem lab, and a proportion of the material on sale, could be considered unhealthily morbid, if not downright malevolent. Should we be subjecting our children to this? Is this truly what an advanced society looks like? Extraordinary. Given that most of this stuff is manufactured overseas, I have often wondered what other cultures make of it – and us; I am sure it encourages widespread respect. You even hear people, crassly, wish one another "Happy Halloween". Really?! Of course, it is all a consequence of unregulated capitalism; that is not a criticism, just a statement of fact. Like many other high days and holidays, today's Halloween is big business and owes much to the same inspired philanthropists that bring us all those other wonderful, sincere, traditional celebratory occasions – like Obscure Relation Moment, International Raspberry Week and Fluffy Bunny Day.

In short, something quite ancient has been hijacked by people who make it up as they go along, purely to make money. Tut-tut. Until Halloween became the jolly time we all know and love, sensible folk would stay indoors and bolt their doors. But like many of us and our customs, it has a confused past.

In the Christian calendar, 31st October is Hallow even, the night of All Hallows, which precedes Hallowmas – or All Saints' Day – on 1st November. 'Hallows' is from the Anglo-Saxon word *halig*, meaning 'holy' – nothing to do with Harry Potter (sorry). So that's where the name comes from; but what's that got to do with all the scary stuff?

Brewer's excellent 'Dictionary of Phrase & Fable', first published in 1870, says, Hallowe'en, "According to Scotch superstition, is the time when witches, devils, fairies and other imps of earth and air hold annual holiday." It goes on to say that those born on All Hallows' Eve are meant to have the gift of double sight and commanding powers over spirits. In my experience, double sight sometimes comes from having no commanding power whatsoever over certain spirits - but that's another matter. In any event, Brewer makes no mention of Christianity and seems to be drawing heavily on Robbie Burns, who a century earlier wrote a poem about it and said that Halloween is:

"The night when witches, devils and other mischief-making beings, are all abroad on their baneful midnight errands; particularly those aerial people, the Fairies, are said on that night to hold a grand anniversary."

31st October was (or is) the feast of Samhain (I'm told this is pronounced sah-win or sow-en), the last night of the year in the ancient Celtic calendar, and the end of summer with all its lightness and bounty. An ending leads to a beginning; ergo, it additionally marks the start of winter, cold and black as the grave. The walls between our world and the next are thin and porous at this time, so this is when the spirits of the departed can most easily move amongst us, as can other phantoms, ghouls, spectres and banshees. Therefore, Samhain is also the Feast of the Dead, a propitious time for witches and warlocks to hold particular rituals. Bonfires would be lit to help the sun on its way through the chill dark months ahead; perhaps the occasional, innocuous, sacrifice would be made.

Later, when Christianity came along, someone decided it was a good idea to have an All Saints' Day, when every holy (or hallowed) person could be remembered. There are different ideas as to how and when this came to coincide with the older ritual, but there was doubtless a bit of competition going on. In the 9th century, Pope Gregory IV formally replaced a May festival of Martyrs with the Feast of All Saints on 1st November, possibly to counteract the more established celebrations of Samhain. And 2nd November is All Souls' Day for many traditional Christians, when prayers are said for the faithful departed and those in purgatory.

In some parts of Europe, it was customary to hold a vigil for the souls of close ones no longer in this world. Soul cakes would be baked and, in return for one of those, beggars would promise to pray for the dead of a household. The tradition of 'soul caking' is maintained in parts of Cheshire today, where actors perform a centuries old play intended to protect against the Dark. No doubt the revellers at Samhain would dress up, sporting antlers and representations of spirits – some of them malignant. Some say that that the ancient Celts dressed in white and blackened their faces during Samhain in an effort to fool evil spirits. Nicholas

Rogers, a professor of history at York University, Toronto, even claims that in the Middle Ages "there was a certain degree of cross dressing in the actual ceremony of All Hallow's Eve." 'Guisers' – people in strange masks and costumes – certainly became popular from the 17th century in parts of Britain, going from house to house singing and dancing to keep evil at bay. Perhaps all of this was the origin of 'trick or treat', a phrase that emerged in the USA in the 1920s.

Food offerings may once have been left for the dead, and some believe that's how the lantern made from a hollowed out pumpkin or other vegetable evolved. Carving lanterns from turnips was common in Ireland and Scotland, and exported by immigrants to the US, where the pumpkin is native and easier to cut. Pumpkins were virtually unknown in the United Kingdom until relatively recently. In the US, a carved orange-coloured pumpkin with a light in it is known as a 'Jack O' Lantern' – itself with a legend that probably originated from Ireland. In England, Jack-a-Lantern is an alternative name for 'Will O' the Wisp' – a ghostly light seen by weary travellers at night, or 'friar's lantern' – an *ignis fatuus* (fatuous fire). Interestingly, my chum Brewer says that there is a Russian superstition that "these wandering fires are the spirits of still-born children which flit between Heaven and the Inferno." Carved lanterns in windows would perhaps ward off evil – or perhaps guide the spirits. In Somerset, some villages celebrate Punkie Night on the last Thursday of October – 'spunkie' is an old word for lantern.

In short, Halloween is a mish-mash of myths and legends from all over, a cocktail of beliefs and rituals which have been exported to other lands, particularly the USA, and re-imported. US servicemen stationed in Europe during World War II brought their hybrid traditions with them, ideas spread further, and gradually evolved, via films and TV. When I was growing up in England – oh, a very long time ago – Halloween was a night for staying under the blankets;

bonfires and masks were reserved for 5th November, Guy Fawkes' Night. Nobody went trick or treating in any big way until the 1980s - but they did in Scotland, where it is still often called guising.

Anyway, when the kids coming knocking on the door yelling, "Trick or treat?", remind them that they are taking part in the latest manifestation of rituals that go back to a time out of mind. Or you could say that they are the victims of someone's marketing plan and greet them, as I do, wearing a ghoulish mask. Of course, it's just a bit of harmless fun…isn't it?

The good news is that being frightened is beneficial for you, allegedly: fear gets adrenaline pumping, helping to relieve depression and stress, whilst at the same time boosting the immune system – and the libido. So put on a scary movie and have a really good night.

# 11
# GUY FAWKES' NIGHT
## 5 November

 As darkness falls on or around 5th November, bonfires splutter to life in back gardens and parks, fireworks whoosh and burst in the sky and a slightly acrid smoke hangs about the autumnal air. Guy Fawkes' Night, also known as 'Fireworks' Night', or 'Bonfire Night', stems from an Act of Parliament of 1606 that declared November 5 an annual occasion of national thanksgiving for the discovery and thwarting of the Gunpowder Plot, or 'Gunpowder Treason', the previous year. The plot was an English Roman Catholic inspired conspiracy to blow up the Houses of Parliament in London on November 5th 1605, the opening day of a new session, and stage a coup d'état. Guido (or Guy) Fawkes was not the leading conspirator, but the bloke caught in the wrong place, loitering suspiciously in an undercroft beneath Parliament, where enough gunpowder – 36 barrels - had been stashed to blast the place above and everyone in it, including the King, sky high. It would have been dreadful carnage – statistically worse than the terrorist attacks in London of 2005 – probably hundreds would have died. The Act of Parliament marking the celebration was repealed in 1859, but the event is still marked, though nowadays often overshadowed by the more commercially exploited Halloween. It used to be common to see children dragging round home-made lumpy effigies of Guy Fawkes in the days leading up to his special night and asking, "A penny for the guy, Mister?". In theory, the accumulated pennies went toward the purchase of fireworks and the poor effigy would be burned on its pyre. Burning effigies is not always considered appropriate behaviour in 21st century Britain and costs and safety

concerns have encouraged more organised firework displays at the expense of smaller domestic affairs. Effigies are still burned, however, perhaps most notably at one of Britain's best-known bonfire celebrations in Lewes, East Sussex, where a number of societies parade through the streets and stage their own displays. The Lewes event additionally commemorates seventeen Protestants from the town burned to death during the reign of Queen Mary (1553-58) and the effigies include topical figures of arguably popular derision.

What on earth happened more than 400 years ago to bring this potential mayhem about?

Since the 15th century Reformation, it wasn't easy being a Roman Catholic in Protestant Britain. Your very way of life was threatened. You couldn't practise your religion openly and there was the constant danger of arrest, or worse. The issue for the authorities, aside from any difference over religious dogma, was plain and simple – it was one of divided loyalties. Could Catholics, bound to obey the Pope in Rome, and sharing a religion with England's enemies, France and Spain, be loyal to the English Crown? It was partly the fault of Pope Pius V, who had excommunicated Queen Elizabeth in 1570 – effectively making her a legitimate target for assassination by any maverick Catholic and having a catastrophic effect on Catholics as a whole in England by turning every one of them into potential traitors. Indeed, there were plots against Elizabeth – which were ruthlessly put down. The new King of England in 1603, James I, had as King James VI of Scotland, allegedly suggested that things would be easier for Catholics if – or when – he became king of both countries. And, of course, things didn't get easier at all – partly because of two plots to remove James from the throne early in his reign.

To cut a long and fascinating story very short, a charismatic and prominent Catholic, Robert Catesby, decided he'd had enough and assembled a band of like-minded souls to 'make a blaze'. They met in the gatehouse of the Catesby family home at Ashby St Ledgers, Northamptonshire. There were five initial conspirators - Catesby, Thomas Wintour (or Winter), Thomas Percy, John Wright and Guy (or Guido) Fawkes. Later recruits were Robert Wintour (brother of Thomas), Christopher Wright (brother of Thomas), Francis Tresham, Robert Keyes, John Grant, Thomas Bates, Ambrose Rookwood and Sir Everard Digby. A baker's dozen. Catesby's ambitious plan included a rebellion based in the English Midlands, kidnapping the King's daughter, Elizabeth, and making her queen – having just blown up her dad and possibly other family members too – and all with the active support of the Spanish. In short, this was to be what is these days euphemistically termed 'regime change'. Ironically, however, Anglo-Spanish relations were improving and a peace treaty was signed in August 1604; the conspirators would receive no help from Spain. There were a number of Catholics in parliament who were loyal to the King – or, at least, recognised that it was not in their best interest to rock the boat. One of them, Lord Monteagle, received a mysterious anonymous letter, warning him not to attend parliament when it opened on November 5th 1605. He promptly took the letter to the King's chief minister and spymaster, Lord Salisbury, Robert Cecil. Parliament was searched – twice. Fawkes was captured late in the night on 4th or early in the morning of 5th November and, following discovery of the gunpowder and his refusal to reveal any details of the plan, subsequently tortured in the Tower of London – probably using the rack. The plot was obviously foiled but, despite that, Catesby still thought he could raise support amongst other dissident Catholics. Incidentally, to this day, no one knows who wrote the Monteagle Letter, though some believe the culprit was Francis Tresham, who happened to be Monteagle's brother-in-law. Another theory is that the devious Robert Cecil himself was behind it, as part of a wider plan to discredit Catholics.

Most of the plotters fled London once Fawkes' arrest was known, heading for the Midlands, where many were based and where the next phase of the plot, the kidnap of the King's entirely innocent daughter, was due to take place. Six of them met up at Ashby St Ledgers for the last time on the night of the 5th, before proceeding to Dunchurch, near Rugby, where they assembled with others. Catesby tried to persuade his colleagues that they could still win through by raising a Catholic rebellion; and, such was the man's persuasive and engaging personality that many believed him – or were simply very dedicated friends. Like the majority of fanatics, Catesby was detached from reality; most people were loyal to the Crown – or simply did not want to get involved. Eventually, seven of the main insurgents ended up at Holbeache House in Staffordshire – these days, it's a care home. Here, several of them were badly burned – including Catesby – when some of their gunpowder was ignited by a spark from a fire. One, John Grant, was blinded. On 8th November, the Sheriff of Worcester, Richard Walsh, lay siege with 200 men. In the ensuing gun battle, Robert Catesby, Thomas Percy and brothers Christopher and John Wright were killed. The rest were overcome and other plotters and associates rounded up and interrogated one by one as the (possibly understandably) paranoid government investigation gained pace.

The dead insurgents – including Catesby - were the lucky ones. Francis Tresham, perished – probably of a natural medical condition - in the Tower of London on 22nd December. The remaining plotters were found guilty of treason and sentenced to be hanged, drawn and quartered. Before this terrifying death, they were dragged, feet first, on a wooden trestle through the streets of the capital. The horrific sentences were carried out in batches: on 30th January 1606, Thomas Bates, Robert Wintour, John Grant and Sir Everard Digby were executed in St Paul's Churchyard; Thomas Wintour, Robert Keyes, Ambrose Rookwood and Guy Fawkes were executed in Old Palace Yard, Westminster, the following day. Their heads, and those of Catesby and the others who had died earlier, were removed and exhibited on poles.

They were not the only victims of the Gunpowder Plot – their families suffered, others were implicated, questioned, imprisoned, fined and at least one, Father Henry Garnet, a Jesuit priest, was gruesomely executed too. The legacy of the Gunpowder Plot, though, haunted Catholics, and the United Kingdom, down the years - not least in helping to spin out religious intolerance; it is not as simple as the superficially innocent British tradition of lighting a bonfire and setting off a few fireworks every 5th November.

*Remember, remember the fifth of November*
*The gunpowder treason and plot.*
*I see no reason why gunpowder treason*
*Should ever be forgot.*

Had the plan succeeded, many innocent people would have died – and, perhaps, if the terrorists' hopes had been realised, Britain's story would have taken a different path. By the way, the Yeomen of the Guard still search the cellars underneath the Houses of Parliament just before the State Opening.

# 12
# ARMISTICE DAY
## 11 November

Armistice Day, or Poppy Day, commemorates the armistice signed between the Allies, Britain and France, and Germany bringing an end to hostilities on the Western Front in World War I. The armistice took effect at eleven o'clock in the morning – "the eleventh hour of the eleventh day of the eleventh month" in 1918. Armistice Day has been commemorated on 11th November since the first anniversary of the end of the First World War, in November 1919, when the custom of a two-minute silence at 11am began. For many years, work came to a halt, traffic would stop and people would stand in silent remembrance.

After the Second World War, commemorations switched to the second Sunday in November – Remembrance Sunday – a day when all of those who had died in conflicts around the world would be remembered, a practice observed by other nations. Armistice Day itself is still observed in the UK, but the major commemoration is on Remembrance Sunday.

One of the legacies of the First World War was the construction of war memorials, in the towns and villages, and even workplaces, of combatant nations all round the world. It was a unique phenomenon. Some, like the memorials to the missing at Thiepval in France, or Ypres' Menin Gate in Belgium, are huge, and humbling. Local memorials more modestly commemorate the young men who left and never returned to their communities. There are around 100,000 such war memorials in Britain, but the focus of national remembrance is the Cenotaph – 'empty tomb' in Greek – in the middle of Whitehall in London. It was designed by Sir Edwin Lutyens, initially in wood and plaster for the victory parade in July 1919, but was completed in Portland Stone in time for King George V to unveil it at the second Armistice Day in 1920. It is intentionally neutral, devoid of any image, name, or religious iconography, so that all troops and people can share it.

Another feature of national remembrance introduced in 1920 was an inspired piece of symbolism, the tomb of the Unknown Warrior. It is just inside the west door of Westminster Abbey, the first detail seen by anyone entering that way, a slab of black Belgian marble beneath which lie the remains of a randomly selected unidentified British servicemen from the battlefields of the Western Front. His coffin was made with oak from a tree grown in the grounds of Hampton Court Palace and he was buried with great ceremony that Armistice Day in soil taken from the battlefields. The inscription on the marble reads:

BENEATH THIS STONE RESTS THE BODY
OF A BRITISH WARRIOR
UNKNOWN BY NAME OR RANK
BROUGHT FROM FRANCE TO LIE AMONG
THE MOST ILLUSTRIOUS OF THE LAND
AND BURIED HERE ON ARMISTICE DAY
11 NOV: 1920, IN THE PRESENCE OF
HIS MAJESTY KING GEORGE V
HIS MINISTERS OF STATE
THE CHIEFS OF HIS FORCES
AND A VAST CONCOURSE OF THE NATION
THUS ARE COMMEMORATED THE MANY
MULTITUDES WHO DURING THE GREAT
WAR OF 1914-1918 GAVE THE MOST THAT
MAN CAN GIVE LIFE ITSELF
FOR GOD
FOR KING AND COUNTRY

FOR LOVED ONES HOME AND EMPIRE
FOR THE SACRED CAUSE OF JUSTICE AND
THE FREEDOM OF THE WORLD
THEY BURIED HIM AMONG THE KINGS
BECAUSE HE
HAD DONE GOOD TOWARD GOD AND
TOWARD
HIS HOUSE

The tomb of the Unknown Warrior was the idea of the Reverend David Railton, who had seen a grave in France marked with a cross and the crudely pencilled words: "An Unknown British Soldier". It could have been anyone's husband, sweetheart, son, or brother. So many of the dead of the First World War have no known grave; so far as their relatives were concerned, they had simply disappeared off the face of the earth. The Unknown Warrior gave bereaved families somewhere to grieve; they could believe that this was their loved one. During the week following the burial, it is said that that 1.25 million people visited the grave.

In the days leading up to Armistice Day, people start wearing red paper poppies or, perhaps, enamelled poppy broaches. The red remembrance poppy was adopted by the Royal British Legion, the armed forces charity, in 1921 and it distributes upwards of 40 million poppies each year in the UK. Poppies grew in abundance on the battlefields of the Western Front, a fact recognised by Lieutenant Colonel John McCrae, a Canadian doctor, in his 1915 poem, 'In Flanders Fields' after witnessing a friend killed by an artillery shell.

*In Flanders fields the poppies blow*
*Between the crosses, row on row,*
*That mark our place; and in the sky*
*The larks, still bravely singing, fly*
*Scarce heard amid the guns below.*

*We are the Dead. Short Days ago*
*We lived, felt dawn, saw sunset glow,*
*Loved and were loved, and now we lie*
*In Flanders Fields.*

## Remembrance Sunday

The annual National Service of Remembrance is held in London's Whitehall on Remembrance Sunday, the second Sunday in November. Thousands normally attend every year; thousands watch it on TV; thousands more join similar, albeit slightly simpler, services throughout the United Kingdom - and beyond. It is an occasion for everyone to remember and reflect upon service personnel who have died and suffered in the service of their country, and civilians who have been victims of conflict, from all nations.

The National Service is an indispensable part of Britain's calendar. Amazing, moving, humbling and impressive, it has followed a similar pattern for decades, runs like a well-maintained, efficient, machine and gives a unique insight to aspects of the Nation's past and present. The service is open to the public and people attend from all over the world. It is necessary to get there early – probably before 8am – at the Parliament end of Whitehall (Westminster tube station). Take something to drink and eat. Security is a sad reality: roads are closed, entrance to Whitehall is via airport style security gates, there are men on rooftops and police line the barriers. There is also plenty of banter.

Nothing much happens before about half-past ten, when massed military bands and troops of service personnel - Royal Marines, Royal Navy, Guards' Regiments, the Blues and Royals, Royal Air Force – enter Whitehall and form up by the Cenotaph. The bands play traditional music – 'Rule Britannia', 'Men of Harlech', the intensely moving 'Nimrod' from Elgar's Enigma Variations. The crack of a field gun on Horse Guards Parade and the first chime of Big Ben mark the start of the two minutes silence. People are lost in thought. The end of the silence is signalled by a bugler playing the Last Post. Wreaths are then laid at the Cenotaph: the Royal Family, politicians, leaders of Britain's Military and Civilian Services and High Commissioners representing members of the Commonwealth, most of them members of Britain's former Empire. The service is also attended by leaders of all Britain's main faith communities – Protestant, Catholic, Greek Orthodox, Jewish, Muslim, Hindu, Sikh and more, as well as by former prime ministers. There is a short service: and then it is the turn of the veterans, normally thousands of them, from all walks of life, from all over Britain and overseas and representing every conceivable branch of military and civilian service. Their memories are of recent conflicts as much as those of years ago. It is a sobering thought that Britain's war dead lie in 153 different countries around the world and these men and women reflect that global experience. So they march, proud and ramrod straight; some need sticks; some need chairs; some need help. As each group passes the Cenotaph, a member of their party hands over a wreath to be laid at its foot and they turn eyes left and salute. Their medals glint in the sun; who knows what images are in their minds. They and their fallen comrades had been through things that most of us hopefully never will, and can never fully comprehend. To misquote the poem by John Maxwell Edmonds, "They gave their tomorrows for our todays".

# 13
# ST ANDREW'S DAY
## 30 November

 As well as being Scotland's national saint, St Andrew is the patron saint of Amalfi, Barbados, Greece, Romania, Russia, the Ukraine, singers, spinsters, would-be mothers, fishmongers and fishermen, gout and sore throats. According to the Scottish Government's website, St Andrew's Day "is usually marked with a celebration of Scottish culture, including dancing, music, food and drink, with parties going on long into the cold winter night." This smacks of propaganda; the present Mrs Britain, a proud Scot, has never celebrated St Andrew's Day and can't recall any of her countrymen doing so. I have never known a Scot that celebrated St Andrew's Day, either – though many must do, if only because that's what the Scottish Government says. Anyway, let's press on…

**Who was St Andrew?**
Unlike George, David and Patrick, St Andrew is a real celebrity saint. He was of course the first of the twelve apostles and St Peter's older brother. He was born, sometime in the 1st century, in Bethsaida, a lost city or village that once stood on the northern shores of the Sea of Galilee in Palestine, now Israel. According to the Gospel of Matthew, Jesus was walking along the shore of the Sea of Galilee when he saw Andrew and Peter fishing and invited them to become his disciples and "fishers of men." The Gospel of John tells a slightly different story; in this, Andrew was a disciple of John the Baptist before being a follower of Jesus and introduced his brother to Christ, saying, "We have found the

Messiah" (John 1:41). John also suggests that Andrew may have identified the means with which to feed the five thousand. When Jesus was confronted by that great company and asked, "Whence shall we buy bread, that these may eat?" Andrew helpfully said to him, "There is a lad here, which hath five barley loaves, and two small fishes: but what are they among so many?" (John 6:9).

The apocryphal Acts of Andrew, said to be written in the late 2nd/early 3rd century, say that Andrew travelled around Anatolia and the Black Sea area, to Byzantium, Thrace, Macedonia and other lands, preaching and performing miracles, until he finally ended up in Patras, Greece. Here, because he refused to stop preaching the Christian message, and because he also denied the Roman gods, Andrew was sentenced to death. The story is that he was crucified, by his own request, on a diagonal cross, and roped to it rather than nailed, because he deemed himself unworthy to be crucified in the same manner as Jesus had been. Some claim that Andrew actually died on an olive tree and the cross was a later medieval invention, the X representing the first letter of the Greek word for Christ, Christos. Anyway, the date of Andrew's crucifixion is traditionally 30th November 60AD and the diagonal cross, crux decussate, or saltire, is now commonly known as a cross of St Andrew.

### Why is St Andrew the patron saint of Scotland?

Unlike St George, whose selection as patron saint of England appears to have been fairly random, at least some effort has been made to link St Andrew with Scotland. The popular tale goes that St Andrew's remains were preserved at Patras and, in the 4th century, the guardian of them was a monk called Regulus, or Rule. Regulus had a vision in which an angel told him that the apostle's relics would be whisked off to Constantinople (Istanbul), so he decided to hide some of them before anyone could say 'pantechnicon'. Sure enough, shortly after he'd done that, the Emperor Constantius II ordered that St Andrew should be moved to the capital. Regulus then had a second vision, in which he was told to take the saint's remaining bones onto a ship and head west, to the very ends of the earth, until he was shipwrecked; and there he should build a shrine to the saint. So, Regulus set sail and eventually came ashore in what is now Scotland, on the headland of Fife Ness, anciently known as Muck Ross, in the village of Cennrigmonaid, or Kilrymont, which later became the town of St Andrews. And there, the saint's relics – three fingers of his right hand, part of an arm, a kneecap and a tooth – were re-interred. I bet, like me, you're intrigued as to why Regulus decided to rescue those particular parts of the saint's remains.

By way of a skeletal update, St Andrew's remaining bones were later removed from Constantinople to Amalfi for safety, to save them from either French and Venetian crusaders, or Turks (I can't decide which). You'll also be delighted to hear that, in 1879, the Archbishop of Amalfi gave an alleged piece of St Andrew's shoulder blade to the re-established Roman Catholic Church in Scotland. Then, in 1969, Pope Paul VI generously donated part of the saint's skull. Both remains are in St Mary's Catholic Cathedral in Edinburgh; so Scotland still has a shrine to St Andrew. It is understood that the other bits of the poor chap's mortal remains, if that's what they really are, have been returned to Patras. And if, in the 21st century, you should inexplicably find the whole business of relocating and venerating bones just a little bizarre, and maybe a tad macabre, that's perfectly OK.

An alternative tale to the Regulus/Rule story is that St Andrew's relics had been collected from Rome (no idea how they got there, sorry) by Bishop Acca of St Andrews Abbey in Hexham, Northumbria, where the saint was already venerated, and brought to Kilrymont by Acca in around 731 AD. There was certainly a monastic community at Kilrymont by around this time: Irish annals record the death of an abbot called Tuathalan, in 747; this community may well have been founded by the Pictish king, Onuist, son of Uurguist, also known as Oengus I, or Angus (ruled 732-761). It is not known whether the monks had any particular saintly or osseous allegiance. The remains of an extravagantly carved sarcophagus dating from the late 8th century, the St Andrews Sarcophagus, might have contained the remains of a Christian Pictish king – or perhaps a saint's relics.

However, given the widespread popularity of saints in the first millennium after Christ, it still isn't clear how St Andrew was chosen, from so many potential candidates, to be Scotland's particular saint. The traditional legend is that, in the year 832, a joint army of Picts and Scots under King Oengus II met an Anglian Northumbrian force under King Aethelstan near what is now Athelstaneford, east of Edinburgh. The night before the battle, King Oengus prayed that his heavily outnumbered soldiers would prevail in the coming fight and St Andrew appeared to the king in a vision, promising victory. The next day, as the two sides faced each other, they saw a curious cloud formation, a diagonal white cross against the blue sky. Sure enough, the Picts and the Scots won a great victory, Aethelstan was killed, St Andrew was declared Scotland's patron saint and the saltire has been Scotland's flag ever since.

It's a great story, which has obvious propaganda value, as well as echoes of the famous legend that the Roman Emperor Constantine saw the symbol of Christ in the sky before his victory at Milvian Bridge in 312AD. Unfortunately, the King of Northumberland in the 830s was someone called Eanred, who we don't know much about. Aethelstan came later, and was from Wessex, not Northumberland; he is generally accepted as the first king of all England, who took the submission of the kings of the Scots, Strathclyde Welsh, Cumbria and the Earl of Northumbria in 927 and then crushed a combined force of Vikings, Welsh and Scots at Brunanburh in 937. So, if the

Battle at Athelstaneford happened, the enemy was unlikely to have been the Northumbrian Angles, or Aethelstan. The Picts under King Bridei did beat the Angles at the Battle of Dunnichen in 685, but no one mentions St Andrew in connection with this.

St Andrew's apostolic heritage would always make him an important figure to the early Christian church. He was widely venerated; there are hundreds of churches dedicated to him - 600 pre-Reformation churches in England alone, apparently. But, sadly, there is no certainty about when or if St Andrew's body parts arrived in Scotland, or the wonderful story of the saltire in the sky. The trouble is, of course, we're into an area where a lack of evidence combined with the great passage of time, healthy doses of religious mythology, vested interest and cynical exploitation, makes the truth a little hard to discern. It doesn't help that versions of the stories appear all over the Internet without qualification, including some websites that you'd expect to be infallible.

It seems we can be pretty sure that, probably in the 8th or 9th century, a cult of St Andrews somehow became established in Scotland centred on Kilrymont/St Andrews. He replaced St Columba, the man credited with bringing Christianity to Scotland – perhaps partly because Columba represented the unfashionable Celtic, rather than Roman Catholic, faction (see 'Easter'). By 11th century, St Margaret of Scotland, Queen from 1070-1093, felt it helpful – or necessary – to institute a ferry across the Firth of Forth to assist pilgrims travelling to St Andrews – incidentally thus founding the towns of South and North Queensferry in the process. The earliest building in St Andrews now is believed to be the church of St Regulus – St Rule's Church – which dates from the 11th or 12th century. An Augustinian Order was established at St Andrews in the 12th century, supplanting the existing order of Culdees (a monastic community with Celtic roots), and work began building a grand cathedral in c1160. Ultimately, this would hold the great shrine containing St Andrew's relics. In the Middle Ages, having a saint's relics in your possession was like winning first prize in the tourism lottery. So it is quite plausible that the legends of St Andrew's relics arriving in Fife, and the appearance of the saltire in the sky, were encouraged, or even (heaven forbid) embellished. Promoting these stories also had a political purpose, in that it helped contest a claim to primacy by the archbishop of York and maintain a separate identity from England. St Andrews certainly prospered, becoming Scotland's most important cathedral town, rivalling Canterbury in England – some say even placing the Scottish burgh on a par with the shrine of St James at Santiago de Compostela in Spain. All that disappeared in the Scottish Reformation, when St Andrews's shrine was destroyed by Protestant iconoclasts.

St Andrew's image, and the saltire, was being used on seals in Scotland from about 1180 onwards. In 1286, when Scotland was ruled by the Guardians of Scotland in the absence of a king, their seal included the words: *Andrea Scotis dux esto compatriotis* (Andrew be leader of the compatriot Scots). Significantly, St Andrew is also referred to as patron of the Scots in the Declaration of Arbroath, the letter the Scottish Barons sent to Pope John XXII in 1320, asserting their independence.

Mind you, the greatest order of chivalry in Scotland is not called the Order of St Andrew, but the Order of the Thistle – though, as patron saint, St Andrew does appear on the insignia. England's equivalent is the Order of the Garter.

### St Andrew's Cross

Today, the Saltire, a white cross on a blue background, is the national flag of Scotland. It can be seen everywhere, every day, from flags on government buildings to cartons of Scottish milk in the supermarket.

The first evidence of the cross being used as an emblem on its own, without St Andrew, was in 1385 when the

Scottish Parliament ordered it to be worn on soldiers' surcoats, though using black rather than the blue we are used to. A white saltire on a sage green background is said to have appeared on the standard of the Earl of Douglas at the Battle of Otterburn in 1388. There is reference to a roll of blue bunting with a St Andrew's cross on it in the accounts of the Lord High Treasurer of Scotland for 1512 and the main flag for the warship Great Michael in 1513 seems to have been a St. Andrew's cross on a blue background. In 1606, King James combined the white saltire on blue with the red on white cross of St George to create a 'British' flag – and the design became official with the Act of Union in 1707. The concept was continued with the Act of Union in 1801 between Ireland and Great Britain when the red saltire on white of St Patrick was added, creating the Union Flag, or Union Jack, still in use today.

'Tis said the saltire can be seen carved into fireplaces, not only in Scotland, to prevent witches flying down the chimney. You will see the saltire all over the world, used by a huge variety of nations and organisations, including Jamaica and the Russian navy; it also featured in the Confederate battle flag of the American Civil War.

## How important is St Andrew today?

Should you visit the lovely town of St Andrews in search of its eponymous saint, you will discover that the loss of Andrew's digits, knee-cap etc have been compensated for by the arrival of a new cult, called golf. Whilst the town has a huge respect for its past, the veneration of St Andrew disappeared at the time of the Scottish Reformation, which had a profound impact on the town and is a story in its own right. The Church of Scotland that evolved from this event not only does not have bishops, but also doesn't really 'do' saints either. And it certainly doesn't do relics. This might explain why seemingly secular events such as New Year (Hogmanay), Burns' Night and certain football matches have generally received more attention across Scotland than St Andrew's Day has.

Ah but, you say, St Andrew's Day is not so much a saint's day as a national day; that's why the Scottish Parliament passed the St. Andrew's Day Bank Holiday (Scotland) Act as recently as 2007, so that everyone could celebrate it. Very true – but banks do not have to close and it is up to each employer to decide whether to make the day a staff holiday. Students at the University of St Andrews are given the day off – but that's a local tradition. Don't get me wrong – of course there are St Andrew's Day events – but it seems like St Andrew's Day, the big holiday celebration, is too recent a notion to have yet become a fixture on most people's calendars. It might be a different matter in other countries. Near the harbour in St Andrews is a stone with a plaque advertising the St Andrew's Society of St Andrews. A search on the Internet revealed absolutely nothing at all for that, and indeed no significant organisation in Scotland whatsoever; but there are plenty of St Andrew's Societies located all over the world, including in Abu Dhabi, Bangkok, Bradford, Hawaii, London, Montreal, Panama, Surbiton and West Australia. Some of these societies are primarily social, with events organised to celebrate Scottish heritage, but others seem to be almost entirely charitable in nature, based on the premise that St Andrew's reputation is of a kind man who helped others. The two oldest societies are The St Andrew's Society of Charleston, founded in 1729, followed by The St Andrew's Society of the State of New York in 1756. Both were formed by people of Scottish heritage for philanthropic purposes.

The real legacy of St Andrew in Scotland, it seems to me, is his flag. And this is a powerful symbol in and of Scotland – arguably far more so than the flag of St George is for England. Indeed, the Scots are often seen as having an acute awareness of their national identity. So, let's conclude by thinking a bit about Scottishness, and what that might include. Here are a few ideas, in no particular order:

Mountains, rivers, glens, bagpipes, kilts, tartans, Harris tweed, claymores, haggis, potato scones, Tunnock's teacakes, deep fried Mars Bars, Irn Bru, malt whisky, ceilidhs, Jimmy Shand, Lulu, Susan Boyle, Jack Bruce, Rabbie Burns, Mary Queen of Scots, Sean Connery, Robert Louis Stevenson, Walter Scott, Ian Rankin, Billy Connolly, television, penicillin, mackintoshes, Adam Smith, Dolly the Sheep, curling, thrift, patriotism, William Wallace, Robert the Bruce, the Loch Ness Monster, rain, beam me up…

# 14
# CHRISTMAS
## 25 December

 Christmas (of course) is the Christian festival that celebrates the birth of Jesus and it is Britain's biggest annual festival. The term literally means 'Christ's mass' but, despite the Christian message, it has become increasingly secular in nature, seen by many primarily as a family time, as well as being observed by those of different faiths and none. Dig not too far and you'll discover that a good part of our Christmas has uncertain, even mythical, origins and, indeed, that some of it necessitates a hefty suspension of disbelief. But, then, Christmas is a magical time. The story of the coming of Jesus, told against a faint soundtrack of traditional carols, with the tang of winter spice in the air and a clear, starlit, sky above, is certainly magical for many.

The angel Gabriel visits the virgin Mary, who is betrothed to Joseph, in Nazareth and tells her she will have a son, who shall be called Jesus. And Jesus shall be the Son of the Highest and reign forever. And then there came a decree from Cæsar Augustus, that all the world should be taxed. And Joseph went to his home city of Bethlehem, the city of David, to pay his tax. He travelled with Mary, who was great with child, and so it was that, while they were there, she brought forth her firstborn son, and wrapped him in swaddling clothes, and laid him in a manger; because there was no room for them in the inn.

In the same country, shepherds were keeping watch over their flock in the field by night. And the angel of the

Lord visited them and said, "Fear not: for, behold, I bring you good tidings of great joy. For unto you is born this day in the city of David a Saviour, which is Christ the Lord. And you shall find the babe wrapped in swaddling clothes, lying in a manger."

Wise men from the east came to Jerusalem, to the court of King Herod, guided by a star in search of he that is born King of the Jews. And Herod sent them to Bethlehem, where the star stood over where the young child was. The wise men worshipped him and gave him gifts of gold, frankincense and myrrh. And being warned in a dream not to trust Herod an inch, they returned to their own country another way.

To many, this will evoke memories of childhood, simpler times, crammed into a cold church with friends, belting out 'Once in Royal David's City', dreaming of no school and Father Christmas. Father Christmas, or Santa Claus, the bearded red-robed figure who visits good boys and girls on the night before Christmas, is the personification of the season for many. Some years ago, when my children were very small, I was dismayed to hear my son pipe up that little Johnny said that his dad had told him there was no such person as Santa Claus. I knew little Johnny's family kept Christmas and wondered how such a miserable pillock could not only undermine his own child's pleasure, but other children's too. How dare he? It being the season of peace and goodwill, I resisted the urge to seek out this idiot and roundly chastise him. Besides, he was undoubtedly a very confused, sad, man. Instead, I painstakingly explained to my son that Santa Claus was magic and, if you believe in magic, then Santa will be real for you. This worked a treat for some considerable time – maybe until my son was in his early 20s.

Santa has little to do with the birth of Christ, yet somehow the two manage to inconveniently co-exist. Actually, a great deal of Christmas has little to do with the birth of Christ. It is intriguing, for example, to imagine some old German or Norseman, arguably long before Jesus was a glint in anyone's eye, introducing the first Yule Log. It was a symbol of fire and light in the dark, cold, northern winter; no one could have imagined it would one day morph into a chocolate-covered cake. Even so, the old Midwinter Festival of Yule, and its log, are both as much a part of our festive tradition as chocolate cake and a whole bunch of other Christmas stuff, including the date.

No one knows which year Christ was born – anywhere between 7BC and 29AD as far as I can make out. And no one knows the date. Some people think He was born in April. Or May. Or June. Or March. But not 25th December. Our heathen ancestors in the Northern Hemisphere celebrated the Winter Solstice around the 21st or 22nd December – and modern pagans still do. The Romans celebrated Saturnalia between 17th – 23rd December. The 25th was *dies natalis solis invicti*, 'the birthday of the unconquered sun'. These festivities could be times of serious merriment – no humbug. Some say that December 25th was also the feast day of another deity, Mithras, much favoured by the Roman military. Incidentally, Mithras is said to have worn a red cap, just like Santa Claus. Maybe he still does. Anyway, as with so many things, Christianity has either been grafted onto, or merged with, earlier traditions. It wasn't until the 4th century that the official date of 25th December was settled – the birthday of the unconquered son and 9 months after the annunciation. Even now, in Britain and other countries with a strong Northern European culture, Christmas iconography often ignores the climate of Jesus' homeland and focuses on winter. But, irrespective of the chosen date and prevailing weather, there's always a bit of Christmas magic waking up that morning: "Oh. It's Christmas! Merry Christmas, everyone!"

Much of our Christmas has been created relatively recently, by the Victorians. Charles Dickens and Ebenezer

Scrooge (clearly, an ancestor of Little Johnny's dad) have much to answer for. Though it is not true that Prince Albert introduced the Christmas tree into Britain, he and Victoria certainly helped to popularise it. In fact, bringing evergreen branches inside for decoration was an established custom long before that. Different trees have particular properties, often sacred, in different cultures. The use of mistletoe, holly, ivy and evergreen fir trees are traditions dating back thousands of years, warding off evil spirits and reminding us of lasting life, though some say that the prickly holly leaves represent the crown of thorns and the red berries drops of Christ's blood. In that case, shouldn't we be saving our holly until Easter? It doesn't matter; it's all part of Christmas magic.

Boxing Day, however, is a Christian custom: in medieval times, this was the day when the contents of alms boxes were distributed to the poor. Giving, though possibly inspired by pagan practices, is also part of the Christian tradition, perhaps started by those wise men – who would surely have asked for a Sat Nav in their stockings if one had been available two thousand years ago. Perhaps they will as the Christmas story evolves. And it probably will – it certainly has so far. For example, the Bible doesn't actually say how many wise men there were – we only assume there were three, presumably because of the gifts of gold, frankincense and myrrh. Yet, we see three kings from orient are in most Nativity scenes; actually, the wise men, or Magi, found Jesus in His house sometime after His birth, not in a stable or barn. Farm animals also figure in most Nativity scenes, yet the Bible is silent on that too. But the story of Christ's birth is a wonderful one; and, for some, a Nativity scene, complete with wise men, shepherds, sheep, cattle, donkey and all the rest, is part of Christmas magic.

Which brings us neatly back to Father Christmas. St Nicholas, the patron saint of children, whose name gives us 'Santa Claus', is believed to have been a real person, but

Father Christmas is a composite of many figures, evolved over the centuries, and comes in many guises. However, many believe that our 21st century perception of Santa Claus, complete with all the trimmings of reindeer and so forth, derives from the poem 'A Visit From St Nicholas' ('T'was the night before Christmas') published just a couple of centuries ago in 1823 and generally attributed to the American Clement Clarke Moore. What do you mean, you haven't read it?! It's part of Christmas magic.

An entire book could be written about the fascinating origins and history of Christmas, as well as the different practises around the world. Suffice to say that customs ancient and modern are embedded in our Christmas and, to be honest, most of them stretch credulity and necessitate the suspension of disbelief mentioned earlier. As a bit of an agnostic, for current purposes I don't suppose it matters which bits are Christian and which bits aren't.

Some people in Britain do not celebrate Christmas, but the vast majority do. When it comes down to it, the fact that the festival, along with all its associated evolving rituals, has been with us for so long is almost humbling. Whatever it means to you – whether it is part of the Greatest Story on Earth, an ancient midwinter feast, a welcome day of relaxation with the family, an over-commercialised stressful time that you'd really rather didn't happen – stop and think about it for a minute. Our parents, their parents, the parents before that – and so on back through the centuries – all marked Christmas in some way. We owe almost all of our present festive custom and practice to people that belong to the ranks of the long dead. And it wouldn't still be with us without a heady mix of faith, story-telling, mystery and enchantment; in short, Christmas magic.

Personally, I find it easy to embrace the whole panoply of Christmas simply because it is fundamentally a Good Thing. There is so much sorrow in the world; Christmas is a time for hope and kindness, for counting our blessings and keeping happy memories of those we have been and are lucky to know. Let's celebrate the rolling year, as our ancestors have done for so long. Let's sing carols, eat cake, give presents, endlessly listen to Noddy Holder, Bing Crosby and all the rest, watch corny movies, play games, fill our houses with tinsel, love, laughter and wonderful smells. And let's not give a fig for whether any of the stories are factually correct, because if we believe them, then they can be; it is Christmas magic. We can also try to mark it as a time of peace in the name of Christianity, for that is our culture and tradition (with a nod on the side to the Old Ones, of course) – or in the name of whatever you like; and if enough people did that, that really would be Christmas magic.

Did I tell you about the Christmas Hedgehog? It was a tiny plastic toy I mischievously introduced into my children's nativity scene and it is now just as much a part of their Christmas as mince pies and crackers. Don't let anyone tell them he doesn't exist.

Merry Christmas!

# 15
# THE A-Z OF CHRISTMAS

 The basics of Christmas are of course ubiquitous in any country with a Christian tradition. That said, everybody celebrates it, if they celebrate it at all, in their own way. Each family has its own traditions, which change over time and as people come and go. Each country has its own unique foibles as well; and, like it or not, Christmas is an ever-changing feast (it always has been). Anyway, this brief guide will help you understand the basics of Christmas in Britain – if you're visiting or if, like me, you've lived here all your life and are still confused.

## A Christmas Carol

'A Christmas Carol' is a short tale, a novella, written by Charles Dickens (1812-70). It was first published in December 1843 and only took the author about six weeks to produce. The story introduces us to the character of Ebenezer Scrooge, a bitter, anti-Christmas, joyless miser, who one Christmas Eve is visited by the ghost of his dead business partner, Jacob Marley. Marley's Ghost tells Scrooge that he will be visited by three spirits. Much to Scrooge's dismay, the spirits - in turn, the ghosts of Christmas Past, Present and Yet to come – do pay a visit. As a result, Scrooge is transformed into a kind benefactor. It is a wonderfully uplifting tale that, personally, I never tire of hearing. There have been numerous film and TV versions, many of them excruciatingly awful; but the very best of all has to be the 1951 film starring Alastair Sim.

## Advent calendar

Advent is the period before Christmas in the Christian

calendar, commencing on the 4th Sunday before Christmas. An advent calendar simply counts down 24 days to Christmas, often in the form of a festive scene printed on cardboard, and with a little numbered door to be opened each day to reveal a chocolate and appropriate illustration beneath. Advent candles are fairly common too, with rings numbered 1 to 24. Advent calendars are not unique to Britain and originated in Germany, where Protestants counted down the days to *Weihnachten* by leaving chalk marks on walls, burning candles or, later, by hanging up little symbols or images each day. The first-known advent calendars as we would recognise them were carved of wood in the 19th century; by the 20th century they were printed on card; the doors arrived in the 1920s and chocolates in the 1950s. When I was growing up, hundreds of years ago, we had a beautiful advent calendar made of cardboard that would be lovingly unpacked and re-used every year; every day, a door would be opened to reveal a little biblical scene beneath.

## Bah! Humbug!

This, normally ironic, expression of disgust comes to us courtesy of Ebenezer Scrooge who trots it out when his nephew wishes him "Merry Christmas". 'Bah!', an expression of contempt, is thought to be French in origin. I once experienced a French mechanic who did a magnificent 'Pah!' of disgust at the intricacies of my old Saab. The origin of 'Humbug', a noun meaning fraud, sham, deception or imposter, is unknown, but dates from the 18th century. One theory is that it derives from the Italian *uomo bugiardo*, a lying man. See 'A Christmas Carol'

## Boxing Day

Boxing Day is the day after Christmas Day and a public holiday. In days long gone, boxes were placed in churches to collect money for the poor and needy. Heads of houses would give small sums to their underlings to put in the box. The boxes were opened by priests on Christmas Day and the contents distributed next day. It was called the 'dole of the Christmas box', or the 'box money'. Later, apprentices would carry a box round to their masters' customers to gather gratuities and it became a tradition to give 'a Christmas box' – what would now be simply called 'a tip' – to those who provided a regular service over the year, such as postmen, dustmen, milkmen, newspaper boys, corrupt politicians and so on. Some people referred to Christmas presents as 'the Christmas box' well into the late 20th century.

### Candles

Christmas just wouldn't be the same without the festive fragrance of paraffin, mingled with cheap, sweet, chemicals, in a scented candle. Lanterns or candles were used in ancient Winter Solstice celebrations as a reminder of light in the darkness and the coming spring, as well as by Christians. Romans gave gifts of white candles as part of their celebration of Saturnalia. Jesus described himself as 'the Light of the World' (for example, John 8:12 "I am the light of the world: he that followeth me shall not walk in darkness, but shall have the light of life.").

Or maybe candles were used because it was dark! They were a main source of light in pre-electric homes and small candles were used to decorate Christmas trees, despite the risk of fire.

### Charles Dickens

We often speak of a 'Dickensian', or 'Victorian', Christmas. Much of our Christmas iconography – cute, snow-covered streets with comfortable looking bow windows, a group of Victorian-clad carol-singers, whiskered gents in top hats, ice-skaters – belongs to this period. We owe some of this to Charles John Huffam Dickens, not just through 'A

Christmas Carol', but his other writings too. The Victorians helped revive a flagging Christmas, at a time when few were in a position to have a particularly happy one. Dickens was born on 7th February 1812 at Landport, Portsmouth, Hampshire and died on 9th June 1870 at his home, Gad's Hill Place, in Higham, Kent. Places associated with him, like the Dickens Museum in London, and Portsmouth, often stage Dickens themed festive events.

**Christmas bells**
It's impossible to avoid bells at Christmas - and who wants to, anyway? Church bells ring out, hand-bells are rung by choirs or in market-places – and, of course, sleigh bells jingle enticingly, but elusively, in the night sky. The song, Jingle-Bells, was written by American James Lord Pierpont and originally published in 1857 as a song for Thanksgiving entitled 'One Horse Open Sleigh'.

**Christmas cake**
A British Christmas cake is normally a fairly heavy, moist, spiced fruit cake, covered in marzipan, then iced and decorated. It should be made about six weeks in advance and regularly 'fed' with a spirit – usually brandy – to add flavour and keep it moist. The marzipan coating comes later and, in my experience, it's often not iced and decorated until Christmas Eve. The decorations often include little model figures – Father Christmas, a robin, snowman, Christmas tree; maybe even a penguin. What?! – you've never heard of the Christmas penguin??

There are regional variations – Welsh, Scottish and English Christmas cakes are all slightly different. In Yorkshire, and to some extent Lancashire, it's considered quite normal to eat Christmas cake with cheese.

Christmas cake and Christmas pudding share a common

origin, a kind of fruity porridge called frumenty, eaten on Christmas Eves long ago. By the 16th century, it became popular to take out the oatmeal, add flour and eggs, and boil the mixture for a cake to be eaten at Easter. The story goes that dried fruit and spices from the east were added to make a special cake to be eaten on Twelfth Night, a traditional time of feasting. Only larger house with ovens baked cakes, though; elsewhere, they would be boiled. Twelfth Night Cake became Christmas Cake as the traditions changed. In some great houses, it was common to bake a dried pea or bean into the cake and whoever got it became King of the Revels.

There is a recipe for Christmas cake at the end of this A-Z.

**Christmas cards**
Even in these digital days, we spend millions of pounds every year on Christmas cards. The first commercial Christmas card is credited to Sir Henry Cole in 1843. Cole (1808-82) was a bit of a Victorian superstar, who helped organise the Public Record Office, assisted Rowland Hill in introducing the penny post in 1840, went on to manage the Great Exhibition of 1851, and was instrumental in the profits from this being used for, among other things, founding the Victoria and Albert Museum, the V&A. Cole thought that sending a generic, printed, Christmas greeting to his many friends would be a lot less laborious than writing individual letters, so he asked a chum, John Callcott Horsley to design one for him. About 1,000 sold for a shilling each (5p now) and the rest, as they say, is history.

**Christmas carols**
According to the Oxford dictionary, a carol is simply a joyous song. However, it was originally an improvised ring dance, to which the dancers added singing, with roots in medieval France, or perhaps ancient times. The tradition of singing at

festivals is surely as old as Man – and certainly not unique to Christianity. Carols could be performed at any time of year – at Easter, perhaps, or harvest-time; so remember, a carol isn't just for Christmas. Equally, hymns are sung all year round; a Christmas carol could be described as a Christmas hymn. In medieval Europe, hymns were mostly in Latin and it is St Francis of Assisi who is usually credited as developing Nativity hymns written and sung in the vernacular, in the 13th century. However, it seems that many carols were not particularly religious and were actually folk songs, sometimes bawdy, associated with wassailing (see 'wassailing'!) and with words that were adapted to suit circumstances.

Christmas Carols as we know them became popular in the 19th century, partly through the efforts of Davies Gilbert (1767-1839) who published 'A Collection of Ancient Christmas Carols, with the tunes to which they were formerly sung in the West of England' in 1822, and William Sandys (1792-1874) with his 'Christmas Carols Ancient and Modern' of 1833 – which between them contain many of today's favourites. Many carols have intriguing origins. See 'Nine lessons and carols'.

## Christmas crackers

Christmas crackers are short tubes of cardboard covered with coloured paper, twisted at both ends, which typically contain some sort of novelty, a joke or wise saying and a paper hat. Two people hold the cracker at each end and pull it apart. A 'snap' runs through the cracker so that a small 'crack' is heard when this happens. The contents then fall out and are kept by one of the pullers. Crackers are normally found decorating dining tables and are pulled before or after the meal; etiquette – including who gets to keep the goodies – varies - though everyone should wear a hat.

It is generally accepted that crackers were the creation of a

London confectioner, Tom Smith, in 1846. Smith was inspired by seeing bonbons (sweets) wrapped in tissue in Paris. He took the idea to England, later adding little mottos, novelties, more extravagant packaging, and the 'snap'.

## Christmas Day

Although Christmas Day celebrates the birth of Christ, we don't actually know when Christ was born. There are many theories why 25th December was chosen to mark the event, possibly by the first Christian Roman Emperor, Constantine, sometime in the 4th century AD. Among other things, 25th December was *dies natalis solis invicti*, to the Romans, 'the birthday of the unconquered sun' – part of the feast of Saturnalia. In Britain, 6th January is sometimes referred to as 'Old Christmas Day'. The calendar changed in Britain in 1752, from the Julian calendar to the more accurate Gregorian. This required a shift of 11 days; so 6th January would have been 25th December in the old calendar. Also, see 'Twelfth Night'.

## Christmas decorations

Until fairly recently, Christmas decorations were relatively modest, with coloured paper garlands and chains hanging from ceilings and homemade tree ornaments. It was unashamedly tacky. Nowadays, increased wealth has allowed tastelessness to flourish beyond imagination, in an apparent desire to light up entire neighbourhoods and outshine everyone else. That said, festive bling can be beautiful and elegant as well.

The practice of festive decoration goes back to at least the great Roman feast of Saturnalia, when temples would be decorated with greenery and little ornaments would sometimes be hung amongst it. The use of branches of evergreen trees reminding our ancestors of everlasting life in the depth of winter, and warding off evil spirits, probably dates back even farther. In Isaiah 60:13, which possibly dates from the 8th century BC, it says: "The glory of Lebanon shall come unto thee, the fir tree, the pine tree, and the box together, to beautify the place of my sanctuary."

The evolution of Christmas decoration is uncertain ground and much of what is written refers to the Christmas tree – a subject in its own right (see 'Christmas tree'). Most sources suggest that trees were decorated with apples in 16th century Germany and that wafers and pastries were then added, with glass baubles and beads first being produced in the Thuringian town of Lauscha in the 1590s. The Germans invented tinsel (lametta), too – originally made of real silver.

## Christmas dinner

There's a fallacy, maybe two, regarding the British Christmas dinner. Firstly, it is often not eaten at dinner time, but during some period in the afternoon between lunch and dinner. That said, the timing is fairly relaxed, in my experience; and quite right too; who am I to remind cook that it's long past the Queen's Speech when she's overdone the port and lemon? (I know, I know, it could be chef, but are you really that picky?) Secondly, you will see reference in restaurants and such to 'traditional' Christmas dinner 'with all the trimmings'; this usually means roast turkey with stuffing, ham, bacon-wrapped cocktail sausages (pigs in blankets), cranberry sauce, bread sauce (maybe), boiled vegetables (typically Brussels sprouts and carrots), roast potatoes and parsnips and gravy. It is usually followed by Christmas pudding, served with cream, custard, or brandy butter. I suppose it depends on when something starts becoming 'traditional' – and I'm probably being pedantic – but the popularity of turkey at Christmas is relatively recent; I mean, the creature isn't even native to these islands. I'm ambivalent about turkey myself; and, anyway, who likes ugly birds? And another thing; while the origins of Christmas pudding are medieval, brandy butter seems to be a 20th century creation, though rum butter, originating in Cumbria, was around in Victorian times. I suppose you could argue – with some justification – that potatoes aren't traditional, either; like the turkey (and cranberries and tobacco), they were brought back from the New World.

It's a personal thing, but I think the only way to eat Christmas pudding is with custard or ice cream (definitely not traditional!). While I'm about it, I would not expect to see Yorkshire pudding served with turkey, as you see advertised on some menus; in my view, it should only be served with roast beef, or on its own with gravy.

Interestingly, there is no 'traditional' starter (aka 'entrée) on the British Christmas menu. In fact, there is no hard and fast rule about a British Christmas meal at all, really – though you'll often find an alcohol-laden trifle offered as an alternative to the Christmas pudding.

The point is, of course, that traditionally Christmas was simply a time of feasting for those that could afford it. And those that could would dine on a variety of dishes; peacock, swan and boar were all widely popular with the idle rich in medieval Britain. Henry VIII is reputed to be the first monarch to gobble turkey, but up to the Victorian era, and before the turkey take-over, the roast of choice was goose.

*Christmas is coming,*
*The goose is getting fat;*
*Please put a penny*
*In the old man's hat.*
*If you haven't got a penny,*
*A ha'penny will do;*
*If you haven't got a ha'penny*
*God bless you.*

## Christmas Eve

Christmas Eve is big news in some countries; less so in Britain, where it is simply the day before Christmas. For the healthily disorganised, it is a time for last-minute shopping and preparation – though many shops and businesses close early.

Even if the Christmas decorations have been completed long before, it is considered unlucky to bring greenery – like holly and mistletoe – into the house before Christmas Eve. My dad used to say that was because It meant that the berries stayed on longer and if I trod one into the carpet it would be very unlucky for me indeed.

Christmas Eve might be a time for carol singing for some and many, even if they are not regular church-goers, will attend midnight mass (which rarely starts at midnight). In recent years, since the 1960s, 'Christingle' services for children have become popular on Christmas Eve. This is an import from the Moravian church. The children make 'Christingles', which are decorated oranges, representing the world. A piece of red ribbon tied around the orange symbolises the blood of Jesus, four cocktail sticks stuck into the orange represent the four seasons and sweets skewered by the sticks represent the fruits of the earth. To round it all off, a small candle inserted into the top of the orange symbolises the light of Jesus. Yes, well.

Christmas Eve is also the time to put out stockings (or maybe pillow cases) at bedtime, just in case Father Christmas decides to drop in. He will only visit if there are good children in the house, and then he might climb down the chimney and leave a present or two. It's a tad awkward if you don't have a chimney. However, it helps things along no end if you leave a mince pie and a glass of whisky out for him (Father Christmas is not subject to drink-drive legislation). If you're feeling especially kind, a carrot and a bowl of water will be appreciated by the reindeer.

Q: What did Adam say to his wife the day before Christmas?
A: "It's Christmas, Eve."

## Christmas fairy

The Christmas fairy is a mysterious figure, often represented by a doll on top of the Christmas tree – though some believe it's really an angel. Most people in Britain probably don't think about it much, but fairies are not always benevolent creatures, and are sometimes quite frightening - though we have become used to the idea of a good fairy granting wishes and being a generally helpful kind of soul. Angels, of course, are normally male figures – and also quite frightening; the Archangel Gabriel visited Mary and told her that she would give birth to the son of God, which must have been pretty scary. Somewhere along the way, fairies and angels have got mixed up, so you had better check yours carefully; angels don't carry wands.

At one time, people used to put a figure representing baby Jesus on top of their tree. Maybe it's better to put a star there, representing the light that guided the wise men.

## Christmas ghost stories

"Whenever five or six English-speaking people meet round a fire on Christmas Eve, they start telling each other ghost stories," wrote author Jerome K Jerome. "Nothing satisfies us on Christmas Eve but to hear each other tell authentic anecdotes about spectres. It is a genial, festive season, and we love to muse upon graves, and dead bodies, and murders, and blood."

The Victorians loved ghost stories, and of course one of the most famous examples is Dickens' 'A Christmas Carol'. But it is said to have been a tradition long centuries before that. Are you sitting comfortably? I do hope not...

## Christmas jumpers

Britain has often flirted with dodgy pullovers. Think of those naff little short-sleeve things you see in photographs of the 1940s and 50s, the dreadful 'tank-tops' of the 1970s and the infiltration of Fair Isle in the 1980s. Even I know it wouldn't be fair to entirely blame fireside crooners, skiers and golfers for every piece of hideous knitwear you've ever seen.

Which brings us to the Christmas jumper. Always a favourite unwanted gift, the 21st century Christmas jumper is in a class of its own. Indeed, this woolly wonder has gone beyond discomforting geometric patterns and embraced kitsch to an extreme that only those who think it's tasteful to festoon their houses with illuminated inflatable nativity scenes can aspire to. The difference, of course, is that the Christmas jumper is generally meant to be ironic. What some experts believe began in 2001 in the UK, when Mark Darcy (Colin Firth) met Bridget Jones (Renee Zellweger) sporting a large reindeer head on his roll-neck, has evolved to a wonderfully ridiculous degree in which garish vulgarity is the new cool at Yule. Attach a few bells and lights, and it is possible to compete with your friends for wearing the most over the top jumper at the Christmas party. With the addition of a compact power supply and a mobile app, who knows where it will end?

## Christmas movies

There have been Christmas movies ever since there has been a movie industry. But, notwithstanding a few classics, it probably took the explosion of video and DVD to bring the genre into everybody's home. Most Christmas movies are American (I was practically weaned on Irving Berlin's 'White Christmas'), a reflection of Hollywood's worldwide dominance; but we Brits have produced a few corkers - such as, 'Scrooge', 'the Snowman' and 'Love Actually'. Personally, I'm a sucker for a good Christmas movie and I'd far rather watch a timeless classic than some of the rubbish that's dished up on TV over the festering season. It just hasn't been the same since they stopped doing the 'Morecambe and Wise Christmas Show'.

## Christmas music

Music is huge part of Christmas – not just carols, but popular, festive, numbers too. These seem to drift, uninvited and unwelcome, into my consciousness sometime in October; personally, I think it should be illegal to play Christmas music before December. At one time, every major star, including Paul McCartney and Elton John, was scattering tinkling bells through their festive offerings and, even in this digital download age, there's still tremendous competition for the Christmas top-slot. Britain's best-selling Christmas No 1 of all time (so far) is Band Aid's 'Do They Know It's Christmas?' (1984). Personally, I'm a sucker for 'Have Yourself a Merry Little Christmas' – Judy Garland (1944), but in the home-grown camp it's hard to beat 'Fairytale of New York' – the Pogues with Kirsty MacColl (1988); 'Happy Xmas (War is Over)' – John & Yoko (1971); 'Merry Christmas Everybody' – Slade (1973) and 'I Believe in Father Christmas' – Greg Lake (1975).

## Christmas presents

Received wisdom is that giving and receiving presents at Christmas reminds us of the presents given to Jesus by the wise men. Working in the UAE one year, I was tickled to bring back some frankincense and myrrh from the spice souk, which I boxed up, wrapped in gold paper and gave to the memsahib. In Britain, the practice of buying and receiving Christmas presents is a relatively recent phenomenon and really took off in industrial and Victorian times, particularly in the latter part of the 19th century with the development of department stores. Traditionally, gifts of produce were given at New Year – and the Christmas Box (see 'Boxing Day') was distributed the day after Christmas. Gifts are now usually exchanged on Christmas Day, but there is no established custom and practice regarding exactly when the business should take place. Certainly, younger children are generally allowed to see if Father Christmas has visited as early as mum and dad will allow; but, beyond that, it really is a matter of family tradition and personal choice.

## Christmas pudding

Christmas pudding, sometimes called plum pudding in older cookbooks, is traditionally served on Christmas Day. The ingredients vary slightly from recipe to recipe, but generally include suet, flour, breadcrumbs, brown sugar, eggs, dried and fresh fruit, ginger, spices, treacle and brandy. It is boiled and keeps for months and months...

Once upon a time, people used to eat a kind of porridge, or pottage, (a sort of soup or stew simmered for a long time) on Christmas Eve. It was eaten to line the stomach after fasting for the day, which was customary on Christmas Eve – 'the Vigil' as it was once known. This pottage was called 'frumenty' and was made of beef and mutton with raisins, currants, plums (prunes), wines and spices. Over time, more ingredients were added – eggs and breadcrumbs, which made it more pudding-like – and ale, spirits and more dried fruit was put in to increase the flavour. By the late 16th – mid-17th century, it was a boiled Christmas dessert known as plum pudding – though the republican government of Oliver Cromwell decided it was not fit for God-fearing folk and it took George I to rediscover it. Somewhere along the way, the meat was dropped.

The first reference to Christmas pudding comes in the 1840s

(Dickens mentions it in 'Christmas Carol'). By this time, it was usual to roll all the ingredients into a large ball and wrap it in a hessian cloth to keep everything together while it was boiled. Hence, many early pictures of Christmas pudding show it as a round ball. Some Victorians, though, made their Christmas puddings in elaborate moulds. These days, most of them are pudding-basin shape.

It is customary to put a sprig of holly on top of the Christmas pudding before serving, then drizzle some brandy over the top, light it, and carry the flaming pudding into the room. Another tradition is to place silver coins in the pudding mix (wrapped in greaseproof paper), which are considered lucky and kept by whoever receives them in their serving. In pre-decimal times, silver threepenny pieces were used, then sixpences; these days, the closest equivalent is a 5p piece.

**Christmas tree**
The Christmas tree is descended from the Scandinavian "Yggdrasil, the Tree of Time, whose roots penetrate to heaven, Niffheim and Ginnungagap (the gap of gaps). In Ginnungagap the frost giants dwell, in Niffheim is the great serpent Nidhögg; and under this root is Helheim, the home of the dead". [Brewer's Dictionary of Phrase and Fable].

According to some, the use of evergreen trees, wreaths, and garlands to symbolise eternal life was a custom of the ancient Egyptians, Chinese, and Hebrews. Some trees were sacred to pre-Christian European peoples and survived the arrival of Christianity in the Germanic-Scandinavian customs of decorating the house and barn with evergreens to scare away the Devil. It also reminded them of spring.

The modern Christmas tree is generally thought to have originated in western Germany – though, allegedly, the first documented Christmas tree was in 1440, in Tallinn, Estonia.

Back to medieval Germany, where a popular play around Christmas was about Adam and Eve (Christmas Eve is regarded by some as Adam and Eve Day). A central prop to the performance was a fir tree hung with apples representing the Garden of Eden, and known as a 'paradise tree'. This began appearing in people's homes, where it would be decorated.

Most people think that the idea of the Christmas tree was brought to Britain by Queen Victoria's consort, Prince Albert (of Saxe-Coburg and Gotha). He certainly helped to popularise it, but the first tree in Britain was ordered by George III's wife, Queen Charlotte (of Mecklenburg-Strelitz) in the 1790s.

**Father Christmas**
Father Christmas, Saint Nicholas, Santa Claus, Sinterklaas, Kris Kringle, or whatever you want to call him, is the personification of Christmas for many people. He is an intriguing figure and a fusion of fact and faction. Contrary to what you might hear, he was not invented by a smart ad-man at Coca-Cola.

St Nicholas, 'Santa Claus', the patron saint of children (as well as of sailors and pawnbrokers), was a real person. He was a 4th century bishop of Myra in the Byzantine Empire (now in modern Turkey), is reputed to have worn red robes and was renowned for his anonymous generosity. One story has him dropping coins down chimneys, where they conveniently popped into stockings drying by the fire. In pagan times, a 'King Winter' figure would have had a central role in festivities; and then there was the Norman red-robed 'Lord of Misrule', whose job was to ensure the Christmas party went with a swing. In Reformation Britain, saints were not universally popular and the less Catholic figure of Father Christmas evolved. He, in turn, was deemed too 'Popish' during the years of the Republic Commonwealth (1649-

1660) – though joy made a come-back after the restoration of the monarchy. Father Christmas has had a variety of robes too – sometimes green, sometimes tan. However, as said above, many believe that our 21st century perception of Santa Claus, complete with reindeer and an arrival on Christmas Eve, derives from the poem 'A Visit From St Nicholas' ('T'was the night before Christmas') published as recently as 1823 and generally attributed to the American Clement Clarke Moore.

Rarely found in Britain, but you may stumble across reference to the Yule Swain, a kind of Santa Claus in Lapland (apparently). He rides a goat, is eleven feet high, appears on St Thomas's Day (the Winter Solstice) and disappears on Christmas Eve. No one knows where he comes from, or where he goes.

**Feast of Stephen**
St Stephen was the first Christian martyr. He was stoned to death in around 34 AD and his feast day is 26th December.

**Figgy pudding**
Figgy pudding is a Christmas pudding made with figs. Surprise, surprise. It is a discrete recipe, though, which any respectable householder will find in their copy of Mrs Beeton's Book of Household Management, first published in 1861.

**Holly and ivy**
Here again we are reminded of the ancient rites we celebrate each Christmas. Holly was used by the Romans to decorate their homes during Saturnalia, and they would send sprigs to friends to wish them health and well-being. Ivy has been regarded as a symbol of everlasting life for centuries and was sacred to Bacchus, the Roman god of wine, and Osiris, the Egyptian judge of the dead. Some associate holly with male

and ivy with female; some with Jesus and Mary. Christians have also associated holly with the crown of thorns that Christ wore on the cross, with the bright red berries representing drops of blood.

Some believe that ivy should not be used inside the house for decoration – and I have certainly never seen it, though Christmas would not be the same without some holly about the place (not before Christmas Eve, though). The carol, 'the Holly and the Ivy', is an old folk hymn – and I have to say that it always sounds very ancient, almost pagan, to me; something about the rising of the sun and the running of the deer...

## Merry Christmas

We can say 'Happy Christmas' or 'Merry Christmas' – but we don't say 'Merry Birthday', or Merry Anniversary' (etc). Does this suggest we don't want people to be joyous on their birthdays? I haven't found a satisfactory explanation for this – not one that doesn't ramble, anyway. 'Merry' is an older word than 'happy' and used to mean 'favourable, pleasant'. 'God Rest You Merry, Gentlemen' (note the comma) is an old carol and the phrase means something like, 'stay well, chaps'. Merry Christmas was used extensively in Victorian Britain - the first Christmas card said, "A Merry Christmas and a Happy New Year to you." But by this time, the meaning of 'merry' had changed to 'mirthful' – and could also mean 'slightly tipsy'. So the temperance brigade may have preferred to use 'happy'. My own fudge on the subject is that it's generally bad English to use the same adjective twice in the same sentence, so if you are wishing someone seasonal greetings for Christmas and the New Year you have to choose a different one for each; and Merry Christmas and Happy New Year sounds better than Happy Christmas and Merry New Year, even though either would be appropriate.

**Mince pies**

There's a theory that eating a mince pie every day over the Christmas period is good for you. I agree.

Mince pies are small round pies with a sweet filling of mincemeat, not – as you may imagine – mincemeat. The mincemeat that goes into mince pies is a mixture of currants, raisins, candied peel, apple, spices, brandy, suet and sugar. The meat component was dropped a long time ago. Originally, mince pies were emblematical of the manger in which Jesus lay, and were shaped accordingly; they became round, allegedly, because the puritans disliked the symbolism (but, presumably, enjoyed the taste).

**Mistletoe**

Mistletoe is a parasitic plant that grows on the branches of deciduous host trees, including oak, apple and birch. The European variety has pale green foliage, long, oval, leaves and clusters of milky-white berries. The Christmas tradition is to hang up a sprig or two and, should a woman stand underneath then a man may kiss her. The mistletoe must never touch the ground, for that brings bad luck. In days gone by, a berry had to be plucked for each kiss and, when no berries were left there could be no more kissing. In these less wasteful times, though, the berries are left on for as long as possible; a wonderful ice-breaker.

The Druids, who practised their religion in these islands before the Romans came, believed that mistletoe was sacred and had magical, healing, properties. Apparently, it really does – though, confusingly, the berries can be deadly poisonous, so do not eat them. There is, inevitably, an association with fertility; it has even been suggested that the berries were associated with semen. It's anyone's guess how the kissing started, though...

Legend has it that the god Balder, son of Odin and Frigg, was killed by a mistletoe arrow given to his blind brother, Hoder, by Loki, the god of mischief. Balder was restored to life but Frigg determined that mistletoe should never again be an instrument of evil, until it touched the earth.

The name mistletoe comes from the Anglo-Saxon word for dung, *mistel*, and twig, *tan*, reflecting the observation that the plant is propagated by birds eating the berries and depositing their waste on the branches of trees.

## Nativity plays

A Nativity play (from the Latin *nātīvitas*, meaning birth) tells the story of the birth of Jesus and is a common feature of any decent primary school's Christmas calendar. It usually features the shepherds, wise men, the fully booked innkeeper and a cast of animals ranging from the donkey to sheep and cows. In the 2003 film, 'Love Actually', they even remembered the Christmas lobster and octopus, which some versions of the Gospels omit to mention. It's a wonderful opportunity for kids to perform, and all to be involved, though competition for the parts of Joseph and Mary can be fierce. I remember being intensely jealous of the toe-rag that got to hold Mary's hand, and was only slightly mollified by winning the coveted role of 2nd Centurion.

Legend has it that the first Nativity play was performed by St Francis of Assisi, in a one-man show to bring the story to life for people who could not read or write.

## Nine lessons and carols

The carol service we are most familiar with today, the 'Festival of Nine Lessons and Carols', which tells the story of the Nativity interspersed with Christmas carols, was the creation of Edward White Benson (1829-1896), in 1880 when he was the first Bishop of Truro and Truro Cathedral was little more than a wooden shed. Benson went on to become Archbishop of Canterbury. The best-known form of that service was adapted by Eric Milner-White (1884-1963) at King's College, Cambridge, and was first held on Christmas Eve in 1918. It is now broadcast around the world every Christmas.

## Noël

Noël is French for Christmas, derived from the Latin *natalis* - birthday. However, noel is also an old English term for a carol, apparently derived from *nowells*, or *nouvelles*, meaning 'news' or 'tidings'. This explains the first noel.

## North Pole

We're not really sure where Father Christmas (aka Santa Claus etc) lives, but a 19th century American cartoonist, Thomas Nast, suggested it might be the North Pole. No one knows where Thomas got his inside information from, but he possibly reached this conclusion from the knowledge that Santa's reindeer lived somewhere northern and very cold, coupled with the fact that the North Pole is nicely remote and receives few visitors.

## Pantomime

Pantomime is a uniquely British - some might even say English – form of seasonal entertainment. Based on a simple plot in which the goodies always win, such as a fairy story like 'Jack and the Beanstalk' or 'Cinderella', it relies on skilful ham acting, audience participation, bad – and often topical – jokes, a bit of slap-stick and some singing and dancing. There are a few other essential ingredients: firstly, a pantomime dame, always played by a man, and a principle boy, always played by a girl. Those who don't know any better suggest this is cross-dressing; it is not; the dame is meant to be a parody of a woman and the boy normally looks exactly like a girl. There has to be an outrageous villain, who attracts boos and hisses whenever s/he enters the stage. A fairy godmother is always useful to have around and, if animals are involved (including horses and cows), they have to be played by humans. Though pantos are primarily aimed at children, good ones operate on two levels; we Brits love our double entendre. And you can take that whichever way you like.

Any town desirous of Christmas credibility will have a pantomime running over the festive period (to make up for Parliament being in recess?) and the cast often includes barely-known celebrities as well as classic actors. They may think it's all behind them, but you'll come across amateur productions almost anywhere. Oh yes you will.

The history of pantomime can be traced back to a form of Roman theatre with mime, which evolved into Italian and French street theatre that involved stock characters: the heroine, Columbine, the old man, Pantalone, and the clown, Pierrot. Crossing the Channel, this became more outrageous, bawdy, and then received an injection of British music hall.

## Queen's Speech
The Royal Christmas broadcast is an intrinsic part of Christmas for many in the United Kingdom and the Commonwealth. The first Royal Christmas broadcast was in 1932, when King George V spoke on the 'wireless' to the Empire from a small office at Sandringham. George VI carried on the practice, delivering a Christmas message every year from 1939, through the war years, until his death in 1951. Our current queen, Elizabeth II, has broadcast every year except 1969, and the broadcast has been televised since 1957. As well as reflecting on Christmas, the Queen mentions global, national and personal events which have affected her and her audience over the year. It's usually at 3pm on Christmas Day, by the way.

Some foreign chappie wrote that some Brits – especially older ones - stand while this is going on and even remove their hats. Well, the things you learn about yourself and your country from the Internet; but I can't stop to natter - I feel a genuflection coming on.

## Robins

Why do robins feature so much at Christmas? The short answer is we don't know. The usual explanation is that the robin, Britain's national bird and a bold little thing, is often seen during winter looking for food – and the red breast makes the cheeky chap stand out, particularly against the snow. Now, I'm no ornithologist, but as someone who has turned the odd sod in my time, I reckon robins are ubiquitous all year round.

Some will tell you that robins became associated with red-coated Victorian postmen (nicknamed 'robins'), who brought the Christmas post. Robins were even depicted delivering Christmas cards. Others suggest that a robin protected the baby Jesus from the glowing fire in the stable (I didn't know there was one - did you?) – thus gaining its red breast from the heat. Another tale is that as Christ was on the way to His crucifixion and was, mockingly, given a crown of thorns, a robin plucked one thorn that had bitten deeply into Christ's head and, as it did so, a drop of Christ's blood stained its breast. Or it could just be that red, along with green, is one of the colours of Christmas.

## Scrooge

See 'A Christmas Carol'. The name of Dickens' main character in 'A Christmas Carol' is now in the dictionary, meaning someone who is tight with money, or miserly. It is thought the name may have come from an archaic verb, 'scrouge', meaning to squeeze or to press. But I think 'Scrooge' is almost onomatopoeic anyway.

## Sprouts

The sprout – Brussels sprouts – seem to be an essential part of the British Christmas meal. They are really mini-cabbages. And, like Marmite, you either love 'em or detest 'em. I'm in the latter camp and can't figure out why they are foisted upon us at what is otherwise a reasonably joyous time of year. They smell awful, taste worse and have unpleasant side-effects. Unfortunately, they are very good for you; a single sprout contains more vitamin C than an orange. They originated in the Mediterranean, but are easily grown in northern Europe, became popular in the low countries (hence the name) and common in Britain in the 19th century, when people didn't know any better. The only explanation I can find for the inclusion of this hideous vegetable in our Christmas feast (other than the plot to get me) is seasonal availability.

## St Boniface

St Boniface was born Wynfrid, in Devon, sometime in the late 7th century. By the early 8th century, he was working in Germany, converting the heathen *volk* to Christianity. The story goes that he came across a group of pagans who were just about to cheerfully celebrate the Winter Solstice by sacrificing a young man under Odin's sacred oak. Furious, Boniface picked up an axe and cut down the mighty tree – which was instantly recognised as a divine act demonstrating the power of Boniface's God over the other ones. The astonished pagans understandably wanted to know what they would do for Solstice without their tree. Some say that a fir tree instantly grew where the oak had been, and Boniface urged all to take home one of those; other versions of the story say that a tiny fir tree was already there, a symbol of life growing in the roots of the oak. Thus, it is claimed that Boniface invented the Christmas tree.

## St Nicholas
See 'Father Christmas'. St Nicholas, patron saint of children, sailors and pawnbrokers, was a 4th century bishop of Myra in the Byzantine Empire. His bishops' robes were red and he had a reputation for generosity. St Nicholas's feast day is 6th December. According to Brewer's Dictionary of Phrase and Fable, it became the custom, on 5th December, for someone "to assume the costume of a bishop and distribute small gifts to good children."

## Stir-up Sunday
Stir-up Sunday is the Sunday before Advent. People who are more concerned with puddings than their souls believe this is when Christmas puddings and mincemeat should be made – and everyone in the family should have a go at stirring in the ingredients. That explanation might make good sense, but the expression actually comes from the service for the day in the Book of Common Prayer, which says, "Stir-up, we beseech thee, O Lord, the wills of thy faithful people; that they, plenteously bringing forth the fruit of good works, may of thee be plenteously rewarded; through Jesus Christ our Lord. Amen."

## Turkey
Turkeys are birds native to North America and Mexico. It is said they became popular at Christmas because they provided plenty of lean meat – and for Thanksgiving in the US because they were in plentiful supply. They got their name – allegedly – because we Brits confused them with guinea-fowl, which were imported through Turkey. It might have been worse; we could have called them after Galloping Bottom in Somerset. See 'Christmas dinner'.

## Twelfth night, Twelve Days of Christmas
There's a bit of confusion about this. If Christmas Day is the first day of Christmas (which makes sense), then twelfth

night would be 5th January. But some maintain that the twelve days of Christmas begin on Boxing Day and end on 6th January, which is twelfth night. 6th January is the Christian festival of Epiphany, traditionally marking the arrival of the magi, or three kings, at Bethlehem. The Epiphany meant that the person of Christ was revealed, or manifested, to the magi; today, we use the word in the sense of meaning a great revelation.

Twelfth night used to mark the end of winter and be a time of very great celebration and feasting. It still is in some countries, but it has largely fallen into disuse in Britain, and many of its traditions – like Christmas cake – have transferred to Christmas Day. A Twelfth Cake was eaten at a Twelfth night party and was originally an iced and decorated heavy fruit dough.

A variety of explanations are given for the origins of the song, 'The Twelve days of Christmas'. It dates from at least the 18th century and it's probable that some meaning was attached to each of the gifts – and there are different versions of these. Twelfth Night used to be a time for exchanging presents, so perhaps the song is a folk memory of this practice.

Perhaps most people remember twelfth night as the day when the decorations are meant to come down.

**Wassailing**
Wassail was (and still could be) a mulled ale made with a variety of ingredients, including curdled cream, roasted apples, eggs, cloves, ginger, nutmeg and honey. The word comes from the Anglo-Saxon *wes hael*, meaning 'be in good health' and the practice of drinking wassail from a special cup or bowl to mark the New Year is said to have begun in those pre-Conquest times. Over the centuries, it evolved into a

tradition to go 'wassailing' – essentially, it seems, going from house to house, singing, and getting more and more drunk as the night wore on. Ridiculous. At some point It became a tradition particularly associated with Christmas Eve and Twelfth Night. These days, it's called carol-singing.

## Wenceslas

Who was Good King Wenceslas? Wenceslas was a 10th century Duke of Bohemia known as Vaclav the Good, who was martyred after being assassinated by his nasty pagan brother, Boleslaw the Bad. Wenceslas's remains are interred in St Vitus's cathedral in Prague and he is patron saint of the Czech Republic.

The carol 'Good King Wenceslas' was written in Sackville College, East Grinstead, by its warden John Mason Neale (1818 - 1866) and first published in 1853. The tune is actually a spring hymn, *Tempus Adest Floridum* (it is time for flowering) published in Finland (at that time part of Sweden) in 1582.

## White Christmas

It's all very well old Bing warbling on, as he does every year, about dreaming of a white Christmas; the chances of snow at Christmas in Britain are fairly remote. And that's even allowing for the Met Office's extremely broad definition "for one snowflake to be observed falling in the 24 hours of 25th December somewhere in the UK." It's not unknown, but in Britain snow is more likely in January or February. So what's with all the business of snow, sleighs and all the other arctic paraphernalia? Well, it's because two things came together. Firstly, from the mid-16th to the late 19th century, the whole world was colder than it is now; it was a period known as 'the little Ice Age'. Secondly, this coincided with a revival of the Christmas feast – some might say even the creation of much of the Christmas we know – in the Victorian age. Therefore, writers like Dickens, and illustrators, would have been quite used to experiencing snow over Christmas – and therefore that was the way it was portrayed.

## Xmas
Xmas is simply an abbreviation for Christmas using the Greek letter chi (pronounced 'kye'), which looks like an X and is the first letter of the Greek word for Christ, *Khristos*. The early church used the first two letters of Khristos in the Greek alphabet 'chi' and 'rho' to create a symbol representing the name of Christ, or Jesus.

It is not correct to say 'Ex-mas' – you should say 'Christmas'.

## Yule and the Yule log
Yule is an ancient celebration of the Winter Solstice, from late December to the New Year, and is one of the oldest winter celebrations in the world. The word is older than Christianity; it comes to us from the Anglo-Saxon *géol* and the Old Norse *jól*, but its ultimate origin is unknown. In modern Britain, Yule, or Yuletide, is still used as a term to describe the festive season.

The Yule log was a carefully selected log, or tree trunk, that was lit from the burnt stump of the previous year's log – which had been carefully stored. Thus, there was continuity from one year to the next. It was important to keep the Yule log burning for 12 days (the twelve days of Christmas?) through the shortest, dark, nights of winter. The custom is common, with variations and using different woods, throughout northern Europe. However, today's Yule log, more often than not, is a chocolate-covered sponge cake.

## Zzzz
Zzzz is similar to the noise people often make while snoozing after Christmas dinner.

## RECIPE FOR CHRISTMAS CAKE

From the Main Cookery Book, published in 1929, reprinted 1936.

### INGREDIENTS

| | |
|---|---|
| 12 oz butter | 6 eggs |
| 12 oz sugar | 12 oz flour |
| 12 oz sultanas | 12 oz large raisins |
| 12 oz mixed peel | ½ teaspoonful mixed spice |
| 1 lb currants | ½ teaspoonful salt |

### METHOD

Stone and halve the raisins, chop the mixed peel and clean the currants and sultanas. Mix as for cake method and bake, in a tin 9" across, on the lowest runner, in a slow oven for 4½ hours.

NB – To prepare the cake tin, line the bottom and the sides with two thicknesses of greaseproof paper, and tie round outside a band of brown paper. Both the greaseproof paper lining and the band of brown paper should stand 2" higher than the cake tin.

---

## CAKE METHOD OF MAKING CAKES

All fruit should be cleaned, and if it is necessary to wash it, see that it is quite dry before it is added to the mixture.

Remove the sugar from candied peel. Get as much cold air as possible into the cakes by plenty of beating, as cold air expands in a hot oven.

### METHOD

Beat together the butter and sugar until they are white and like thick cream. Beat the eggs and add them a little at a time, beating each lot well in before more is added. (If added too quickly, the mixture tends to curdle). Add the flavourings. Sift together the baking powder (or cream of tartar and bi-carb of soda), salt and flour, as this not only breaks down any lumps in the flour, but also aerates it. Add this to the eggs etc, a little at a time, 'folding' it in as lightly as possible. (Beating a cake after the flour is added tends to make it heavy, as the flour breaks down the little air cells and lets the air escape). Then stir in lightly the fruit, nuts, etc. If the mixture is too stiff, a little milk may be added; the mixture should just fall easily from the spoon.

To test if a cake is cooked, run a clean hot skewer through the centre of the cake; if the cake is done, the skewer will come out clean and smooth.

Leave large cakes in the tins about 10 minutes before turning out to cool.

---

## ALMOND ICING OR PASTE

INGREDIENTS

1 lb ground almonds
8 oz castor sugar
1 teaspoonful vanilla essence
¼ teaspoonful almond essence
½ wineglassful brandy (or rum)
2 eggs

8 oz icing sugar
Juice of 1 lemon

METHOD
Mix together the ground almonds and sugars. Mix together the flavourings, lemon juice, brandy and eggs, beat well, and add gradually to the dry ingredients, kneading it thoroughly till smooth. Use for icing cakes.
If wanted coloured for fancy decorations, don't use the

yolks of the eggs, but only the whites. This will result in a white almond paste, which will mix better with pale pink, green, etc.

---

## ROYAL ICING

INGREDIENTS

2 lb icing sugar                    Whites of 4 eggs

Juice of 2 lemons

METHOD

Rub the sugar through a hair sieve into a basin, add the lemon juice and the whites of the eggs gradually, beating well together with a wooden spoon till smooth and glossy (if it is to be used for piping, the icing should be stiff enough to stand up in points.

---

Author's note: Firstly, I haven't tried these recipes, so have no idea if they work. Chopped almonds and halved cherries could be substituted for a little of the fruit in the cake mix. Also, some Christmas cake recipes use brown sugar and include a little cinnamon, vanilla essence, black treacle, marmalade as well as some brandy or sherry. It is common to 'feed' the cake weekly with a little brandy or sherry over several weeks, to keep it moist, before finally adding almond paste or marzipan and icing to decorate it. Simply make little holes in the top of the cake with a skewer and dribble the liquid through.

# 16
# BRITAIN'S CALENDAR

What's on, when, in Britain? Over the following pages is an extensive selection of annual events that normally take place from Spring through Summer and Autumn to Winter. Some of these will already be featured on A Bit About Britain https://bitaboutbritain.com/ - it is always worth checking the website for updates and more information. Obviously, it's essential that you check for up to date details directly with event organisers before making a special trip.

# SPRING IN BRITAIN

Spring includes the months of March, April and May. The days get longer and warmer after winter and the countryside starts to burst into life. Think of Spring in Britain as the time of bees – buds, blossom, bluebells, butterflies, birds – as well as bees. But you'll notice loads of daffodils, too. Spring weather in Britain is often calm and dry, with relatively warm days and cool nights. However, showers are common and snow in April is not unknown. It is generally warmer in the south than in the north of the island.

## March in Britain

Heritage attractions open – many heritage attractions that have closed for winter start opening their doors again in March.

**St David's Day** is on 1st March. St David is the patron saint of Wales. Britain's smallest city, St Davids, is named after him.

**Crufts** – Crufts is the world's most famous, if not the largest, dog show, normally held in Birmingham in early March and organised by the Kennel Club. It was founded by Charles Cruft (1852-1938), who was general manager of dog food manufacturer, Spratt's. The first Crufts was held in 1891.

**Cornwall (St Piran's) Day** – 5th March, celebrating the county, whose county town is Truro.

**Shrove Tuesday (Pankcake Day)** - falls 47 days before Easter Sunday, so it is a moveable feast (pun intended). The date will be between early February and early March.

**St Patrick's Day** is on 17th March. St Patrick's Day is a

Bank Holiday in Northern Ireland. Although St Patrick is the patron saint of Ireland, his day is often loudly celebrated in parts of Britain too. It is mostly associated with drinking too much; some places even have parades.

**Durham (St Cuthbert's) Day** – 20th March, celebrating the county and the county town.

**British Summer Time (BST)** – the clocks go forward 1 hour at 1am on the last Sunday in March, making the evenings lighter for longer. The clocks go back to Greenwich Mean Time (GMT) at 2am on the last Sunday in October. Remember which way the clocks go, albeit by borrowing from the US – "Spring forward, Fall back."

**The London Marathon** - The London Marathon is normally held on a Saturday in spring. It was first run on 29th March 1981. In addition to being a top international marathon, the event raises millions of pounds for charities.

**The Ideal Home Show** – billed as 'Britain's longest running exhibition', the Ideal Home Show runs for a fortnight or so, in late March/early April. It was formerly called the Ideal Home Exhibition and was devised by the Daily Mail, who ran it from 1908 until selling it in 2009.

**Mothers' Day** – Mothers' Day, or, more properly, Mothering Sunday, falls in late March or early April on the fourth Sunday of Lent and three weeks before Easter Sunday.

**The Boat Race** – the annual rowing boat race between the universities of Cambridge (light blue) and Oxford (dark blue) takes place on the River Thames around Easter. The first race was in 1829 and it has been an annual event since 1856 (except for during the two World Wars). The first women's boat race took place in 1927 and has been held annually since

1964. The course is 4 miles and 374 yards (6.8 km) between Putney (close to the bridge) and Mortlake (near Chiswick Bridge). It is free to watch, but get there early.

**Easter** – the date of Easter varies depending on which calendar is used, and the moon. The UK uses the Gregorian calendar and marks Easter on the Sunday following the first full moon that occurs after the first day of spring (the Vernal Equinox). Thus, Easter falls somewhere between late March and April. Good Friday is a UK Bank Holiday and Easter Monday is a Bank Holiday in England, Wales and Northern Ireland.

**Maundy Thursday** is the last Thursday before Easter and marks the night of the Last Supper before the Crucifixion. 'Maundy' derives from the Latin mandatum, or 'command', referring to Jesus' command that we should all love one another. The ceremony of Royal Maundy takes place on Maundy Thursday, when the Monarch distributes coins, called 'Maundy money', to senior citizens.

## April in Britain

**April Fool's Day** is on 1st April. Watch out for spoof articles in the news media, or workplace jokes. April Fool's Day possibly dates from the time when 25th March was New Year's Day and 1st April, a week later, marked the end (or height) of festivities and fun (fooling). Another theory is that when the Gregorian calendar was introduced by Pope Gregory XIII in October 1582, New Year's Day changed to 1st January and those who didn't hear the news, or forgot, were called fools. The Gregorian calendar was not adopted by Britain until 1752.

**The end of the tax year** – 5th April. This bizarre date is another hang over from the change to the Gregorian calendar, which Britain did not adopt until 1752, by which time it was 11 days out of synch with everyone else. The old tax year ended on 25th March (old New Year's Day) so to ensure full 365 days revenue, the British Treasury decided the tax year would end on 5th April. And they've never got round to changing it.

**Start of the cricket season.** Cricket, the quintessentially English game, is played all over the UK as well as in top-flight (first-class) cricket nations like Australia, New Zealand, India, Sri Lanka, South Africa, Pakistan and the West Indies. Cricket is a summer sport, played at local, county and international level in the UK, where the season starts around early-mid April and continues until September. The ECB (English Cricket Board) gives details of county matches in England and Wales. Cricket Scotland is the governing body for Scottish cricket.

**Orkney Day** (the feast day of St Magnus) – 16th April.

**St George's Day** – 23rd April. St George is the patron saint of England. Surprisingly, it is not widely celebrated.

**Shakespeare's Day** is also 23rd April, though few mark the occasion except the more commercially-minded in his birthplace of Stratford-upon-Avon. William Shakespeare was baptized on 26th April 1564 and died on 23rd April 1616. His birth date is unknown, though some believe it was also 23rd April.

**Huntingdonshire Day** – 25th April, celebrating the historic county, named for its county town.

## May in Britain

**May Day** – 1st May is traditionally May Day, a very ancient and joyous festival that grey and hung-up officials have tried to replace for centuries, most recently with boring Labour Day. You may find some liberated villages celebrating the original festival, complete with a maypole and a May Queen. The unique Obby Oss festival in Padstow, Cornwall, which starts at midnight on 30 April, is one remnant of the old celebrations. Does anyone know anyone that celebrates Labour Day? Of course not!

**Staffordshire Day** – 1st May, celebrates the county named for its county town of Stafford.

**Early May Bank Holiday** - the first Monday in May is the Early May Bank Holiday for the whole of the UK.

**Well dressing festivals** take place from May to August. Well Dressing is a very old custom, possibly dating back to pre-Roman times, associated with the veneration of springs and water. The dressing of wells and springs, when they are exuberantly covered with flowers and other decorations, is now more or less exclusive to villages in the Peak District of England and the counties of Derbyshire, Staffordshire and Nottinghamshire.

**Highland Games** are held all over Scotland from May to September. These competitions have a long history and include traditional Highland dancing, tossing the caber, hammer throwing and pipe bands – often against a backdrop of marvellous scenery.

**VE Day** – 8th May, marks Victory in Europe in 1945 during the Second World War. There may be locally organised events.

**Somerset Day** is 11th May, in celebration of the county whose county town is Taunton.

**Middlesex Day** – 16th May, celebrates the old historic county, which used to lie to the north and west of London, but which has now largely been absorbed by it.

**Chelsea Flower Show** - The Chelsea Flower Show, organised by the Royal Horticultural Society (RHS) is held in the grounds of the Royal Hospital Chelsea for five days in late May. It is arguably the most famous flower and landscape gardening show in the world, and accordingly attracts visitors from all over the world, as well as celebrities.

**Hay Literary Festival** - The Hay Festival of Literature and Arts takes place over ten days in May/June in Hay-on-Wye, Powys. It includes music and stalls, as well as workshops and presentations by well-known writers. Hay is renowned for its many bookshops and was already known as 'the town of books' before the festival was conceived in the 1980s.

**Glyndebourne** - Glyndebourne Festival Opera is held from late May through to August at Glyndebourne, a country house opera venue near Lewes, in East Sussex.

**The FA Cup Final** – the FA Cup Final is the culmination of a knockout football (soccer) competition involving English and Welsh teams and takes place in May or June. It is reckoned to be the oldest national football competition in the world; the first final took place in 1872 at Kennington Oval between the Royal Engineers and Wanderers; Wanderers won 1-0. The Scottish Cup competition has taken place in parallel since the 1873-4 season, when Queen's Park beat Clydesdale 2-0.

**Whitsunday (Whitsun)**, or Pentecost, falls on the 50th day after the Easter festival and commemorates the coming of the Holy Spirit. Some believe the term comes from the day being a favourite one for baptism and the practise of those being baptised wearing white; others think it is derived from wit or wisdom bestowed from the Holy Ghost. It is a traditional day of festival, including Whit Walks (or processions), dancing and cheese rolling. Whit Monday used to be a Bank Holiday, but has been replaced by the Spring Bank Holiday.

**Spring Bank Holiday** is the last Monday in May in the UK.

**Kent Day** – 26th May and the feast day of St Augustine of Canterbury. The county town of Kent is Maidstone.

**Oak Apple Day** – 29th May, also known as Royal Oak Day, Restoration Day, Pinch-Bum Day and Nettle Day – this used to be a public holiday in England, commemorating the restoration of the monarchy, in May 1660. 29th May was also Charles II's birthday.

# SUMMER IN BRITAIN

Summer includes the months of June, July and August. It is the traditional holiday period, when schools close for several weeks, so places generally tend to be a little more crowded. Note that school holidays vary across the country; Scottish schools break up for summer, and return for autumn term, before their English and Welsh counterparts. Summer in Britain is the warmest time of year. On average, July is the warmest month and June the sunniest, but rainfall has been known to ruin many a festival or fete. Heatwaves are possible and there are generally more thunderstorms in summer than at other times of year. As with Spring, it tends to be cooler in the north and warmer in the south.

## June in Britain

**Dorset Day (the feast day of St Wite)** – 1st June, celebrates the county whose county town is Dorchester.

**The Trooping of the Colour**, marking the official birthday of the British Sovereign, takes place in Westminster, London, normally on a Saturday in early June.

**Devon (St Petroc's) Day** – 4th June, celebrates the county of Devonshire (county town Exeter).

**Wiltshire Day** – 5th June, celebrates the county (county town Trowbridge).

**Sussex Day** – 16th June, celebrates the old county of Sussex, once the kingdom of the South Saxons. The county town is Chichester, in West Sussex.

**Aldeburgh Festival** in Suffolk - The Aldeburgh Festival of

125

Music and the Arts was founded in 1948 by the composer Benjamin Britten, the singer Peter Pears and the librettist/producer Eric Crozier. It takes place from mid-late June in the Aldeburgh area of Suffolk, centred on Snape Maltings Concert Hall.

**Royal Highland Show** - The Royal Highland Show is Scotland's biggest annual agricultural show, showcasing farming (of course!), livestock (well…), food, drink, rural life..arts..crafts – all sorts of stuff. It dates from 1822 and is held in June at the Royal Highland Centre in Ingliston, on the edge of Edinburgh.

**Glasgow Jazz Festival** - The Glasgow International Jazz Festival is held in June in the up-market Merchant City area, an open-air stage in George Square and fringe events in bars, restaurants and hotels nearby.

**The Summer Solstice** - the longest day and shortest night of the year, when the sun is at its highest – takes place on or around 21st June. Thousands of people gather at ancient sites to witness sunrise. The biggest gathering is at Stonehenge, in Wiltshire.

**Shetland Day** is on 21st June, celebrating the Shetland Isles. So is Suffolk Day, celebrating the East Anglian county (county town Ipswich).

**Fathers' Day** – is the third Sunday in June. Don't forget old men need pampering too.

**Glastonbury Festival of Performing Arts** - held most years, except for 'fallow years', over 5 days in late June, at Worthy Farm, Somerset. Tickets sell out in minutes – but going to Glastonbury is perhaps something you should do at least once in your life.

**Armed Forces' Day** is normally held on the last Saturday in June. Find events and get involved on the Armed Forces Day website.

## July in Britain

**British Formula 1 Grand Prix.** The British F1 Grand Prix race has been held annually since 1948, most recently sometime in July at the Silverstone Circuit in Northamptonshire.

**Wimbledon** – the tennis championships at Wimbledon, the oldest tennis tournament in the world and the only major one played outdoors on grass, takes place over two weeks (Wimbledon Fortnight) in early July. People have been known to take the time off work as holiday in order to watch it.

**Hampton Court Flower Show** - The Hampton Court Garden Festival (to give its formal name) takes place in early July and is (allegedly) the largest flower show in the world. It is organised by the Royal Horticultural Society (RHS) and features show gardens, marquees and more along the banks of the Long Water in Hampton Court Park, south-west of London. As well as the obvious exhibits, the show is famous for highlighting home-grown food and cookery.

**Llangollen Eisteddfod** - The Llangollen International Musical Eisteddfod is held during the second week of July in Llangollen, North Wales. The tradition of eisteddfod, a Welsh festival of literature, music and performance, dates from the middle ages, at least.

**Hampshire Day** – 15th July, celebrates the old county of Hampshire, whose county town is Winchester.

**Cambridge Folk Festival** - The Cambridge Folk Festival is a 3½ day music festival, established in 1965, which takes place in July on the site of Cherry Hinton Hall on the outskirts of Cambridge. As well as legends and newcomers in folk music, the festival is renowned for a broad definition of what might be considered 'folk' and has included artistes like Wilko Johnson and Patti Smith in its line-up.

**Tatton Park Flower Show** – the RHS Flower Show Tatton Park is held at the historic Tatton Park, near Knutsford, Cheshire, in late July. It includes show gardens and prize exhibits, as well as young designer and national flower bed competitions.

**Henley Regatta** - Henley Royal Regatta is a rowing event held over five days in late July at Henley-on-Thames, England. First held in 1839, it is a traditional 'social season' event, where strict dress codes apply in certain places. So, a good place to spot people with more money than is good for them.

**Norfolk Day** is on 27th July, celebrating the county (county town Norwich).

**Buckinghamshire Day** is on 29th July, celebrating the county (county town Aylesbury, not Buckingham).

**The Proms** - The BBC Proms, more formally The Henry Wood Promenade Concerts, were founded in 1895 and now take place over an 8-week period from July to September, providing a programme of internationally renowned daily orchestral concerts mainly, though not exclusively, in London's Royal Albert Hall in central London. The Last Night of the Proms in September is a hugely popular event which, though intensely patriotic, is also seen as slightly tongue-in-cheek and attracts people from all over the world.

Tickets for the Last Night in London's Albert Hall sell out way in advance. However, outdoor concerts are held simultaneously in London's Hyde Park, Belfast, Glasgow and Swansea.

## August in Britain

**Yorkshire Day** – 1st August, celebrates England's largest county. The county town – of course – is York.

**Summer Bank Holiday** in Scotland is the first Monday in August.

**VJ Day** on 15th August marks the anniversary of Victory over Japan in 1945 at the end of the Second World War. There may be local events taking place.

**Football season.** The football (soccer) season normally runs from mid-August to May.

**Edinburgh Festivals** - The Edinburgh International Festival is one of several festivals that take place in the City during August. Held since 1947, it aims to offer the best in the performing arts - theatre, music, opera, dance, film etc - from all round the world, as well as talks and workshops. Alongside the International Festival is Edinburgh Festival Fringe, an open access event that includes comedy, theatre, cabaret, children's shows, circus - pretty much anything - and ANYONE can take part. Edinburgh Festival Fringe began in 1947 when eight groups arrived in Edinburgh hoping to perform at the newly formed Edinburgh International Festival but were refused entry. They went ahead and performed on the fringe of the Festival anyway. The Edinburgh Festival Fringe is now the largest arts festival in the world. Beyond the Fringe (as it were), Edinburgh is immensely buzzy during this festival, with street performers on almost every corner.

**Edinburgh Tattoo** – the Royal Edinburgh Military Tattoo is held every August alongside the Edinburgh festivals. It features military bands and displays from all over the world and attracts thousands of visitors from overseas, as well as all over the UK, and takes place against the dramatic backdrop of Edinburgh Castle, overlooking the city.

**Beatles' Festival** – International Beatles' Week is held in late August in and around various venues in Liverpool, particularly the Cavern Club. It features tribute bands as well as acts that are famous in their own right, from all over the world.

**The late Summer Bank Holiday** in England and Wales is the last Monday of August.

**Notting Hill Carnival** – The Notting Hill Carnival is Europe's biggest street carnival and takes place in London over the August bank holiday weekend.

# AUTUMN IN BRITAIN

Autumn covers September, October and November. It is harvest time – watch out for food festivals. This is Keats' "Season of mists and mellow fruitfulness" when the last flowers of summer gradually start to die away, apples are ripe, the leaves turn, and the nights draw in. In fact, though Autumn is prone to falling temperatures and mists, sunny days are not uncommon and early September, in particular, can be clear, warm and bright with flowers. It's by no means guaranteed (of course), but an 'Indian Summer' (an expression probably North American in origin), is a good time to see Britain. That said, storms and high winds are common toward the end of the season.

## September in Britain

**Blackpool illuminations** - Blackpool Illuminations is a spectacular annual light show in the north-west seaside town of Blackpool. The first one took place in 1879. The lights are generally on for 66 days from September to November and stretch over 6 miles along the promenade.

**Royal Highland Gathering** - The Braemar Gathering is always held on the first Saturday in September in The Princess Royal and Duke of Fife Memorial Park in Braemar, Scotland. The gathering dates back at least 900 years, but has been run in its present form since 1832. It is regularly attended by the reigning Monarch and members of the Royal Family, and crowds come to acclaim the Monarch as Chieftain of the Braemar Gathering.

**International Sheepdog Trials** – sheepdog trials are held throughout the UK from February to October. The international trials (and, confusingly, the world trials too) are normally held in mid-September. The International Sheep

Dog Society has a full diary of events on its website.

**Rutland Day** is on 13th September, celebrating the small historic county, whose county town is Oakham.

**Battle of Britain Day** is on 15th September, marking the decisive victory of the Royal Air Force over the German Luftwaffe in 1940.

**Derbyshire Day** is on 22nd September, celebrating the county whose county town is Derby.

**Cumberland Day** is on 24th September, celebrating the historic county, now part of Cumbria, whose county town was Carlisle.

**Westmorland Day** is on 29th September, celebrating the historic county, now part of Cumbria, whose county town was Appleby, then Kendal.

**Great North Run** - the Great North Run takes place in September between Newcastle upon Tyne and South Shields. It is apparently the largest half marathon in the world.

**Harvest Festivals** – celebrations for successful harvests take place all over the world and are ancient in origin. Harvest Festivals take place all over the UK in churches, but also at some farms and parks, usually during September or early October.

**Heritage Open Days.** Open Doors, or Heritage Open Days, during which the doors are thrown open to historic monuments and buildings, in particular those normally closed to the public, take place across Europe in September.

## October in Britain

**Lincolnshire Day** – 1st October celebrates the county on the anniversary of the Lincolnshire Rising of 1536. The county town, of course, is Lincoln.

**Nottingham Goose Fair** - The Nottingham Goose Fair is a travelling funfair that takes place during the first week of October. It dates back to the 13th century, possibly earlier, was named for the geese that were its main feature (doh!) and once had a reputation for its cheese. These days, it is noisy, brash and everything else you'd expect a 21st century funfair to be.

**London Film Festival** – the BFI London Film Festival has been organised by the British Film Institute since 1953. It is the UK's largest public film festival and features more than 300 films and documentaries from all over the world. It normally takes place in the second half of October.

**Battle of Hastings** – 14th October is the anniversary of the Battle of Hastings in 1066, which (as every self-respecting school pupil should know) was a game-changer.

**Bramley Festival** – the Bramley Apple was first grown in the Nottinghamshire minster town of Southwell and the Bramley Festival celebrates this. There's a food and drink fair in Southwell Minster itself and events throughout the town.

**Oxfordshire Day** is 19th October, the feast day of St Frideswide.

**Trafalgar Day** – 21st October marks the anniversary of the Battle of Trafalgar in 1805. It is not widely remembered these days, but you'll hear all about it if you visit Nelson's flagship,

HMS Victory, in Portsmouth.

**Northamptonshire Day** is on 25th October, St Crispin's Day, according to the Government website, but has been recently celebrated in late September. The county town is Northampton.

**Essex Day** is 26th October, the feast day of St Cedd, celebrating the county of the East Saxons. The county town is Chelmsford.

**British Summer Time (BST)** ends at 2am on the last Sunday in October. The clocks go back 1 hour to Greenwich Mean Time (GMT).

**Heritage attractions close** – many heritage attractions close for winter and 31st October is often the last full day of visiting until the following March.

**Halloween** – 31st October. Look out for witches, ghouls and things that go bump in the night. It is also the feast of Samhain (pronounced sah-win or sow-en), the last night of the year in the ancient Celtic calendar, and the end of summer with all its lightness and bounty.

## November in Britain

**London to Brighton Rally** - The London to Brighton Veteran Car Run, the longest-running motoring event in the world, first took place in 1896. Hundreds of cars – all of which have to have been built before 1905 – enter. It normally takes place on the first Sunday in November, starting at sunrise from Hyde Park, London and mostly follows the old A23 road to Brighton 54 miles (87 km) away. It is not a race.

**Guy Fawkes' Night** – 5th November. Guy Fawkes' night (aka Bonfire Night) commemorates the discovery of the Gunpowder Plot on 5th November 1605, when a group of Catholic terrorists attempted to blow up Parliament and launch a coup d'état. Guy Fawkes was one of the conspirators, discovered among barrels of gunpowder in the cellars before Parliament assembled. The modern celebration utilises fireworks. Traditionally, an effigy of Guy was burned on a bonfire, but this is less common now – though effigies still figure hugely at some public events, such as the one in Lewes, East Sussex – which claims to be "the biggest celebrated Fifth November Event in the world."

**State Opening of Parliament** - The State Opening of Parliament marks the formal start of the parliamentary year and the Monarch's Speech sets out her government's agenda for the coming session. It is the only regular occasion when the three constituent parts of Parliament – the Sovereign, the House of Lords and the House of Commons – meet. The event is full of tradition, ritual and symbolism. Though not an open public event, the arrival of the monarch can be witnessed. It takes place on the first day of a new parliamentary session – traditionally in November, but more recently in the Spring, or following a general election.

**Lord Mayor's Show.** The Lord Mayor of London's Show takes place on the second Saturday in November in the City of London. It dates from medieval times and includes an enormous, and varied, procession – which is well worth watching.

**Armistice Day** – 11th November, when 2 minutes silence is observed at 11am in memory of the fallen of all nations. Remembrance services are held all over the country on the Sunday closest to Armistice Day. The National Service of Remembrance is held in Whitehall, London.

**Regent Street Christmas Lights** – among the many streets in Britain, and around the world, that have elaborate light displays as Christmas approaches, London's Regent Street has to be among the best known. The lights are switched on by a celebrity of some sort around the middle of November.

**Lancashire Day** is on 27th November, celebrating the old county of Lancashire, whose county town is (obviously) Lancaster.

**Bedfordshire Day** is on 28th November, celebrating the county named for its county town of Bedford.

**St Andrew's Day** is on 30th November. St Andrew is the patron saint of Scotland, where the day is an official Bank Holiday.

# WINTER IN BRITAIN

Some people find Winter in Britain depressing; the days are short, cold, and many people go to work and return home in the dark. Contrary to Christmas card imagery, heavy snow is rare – except in the high hills and mountains – and the predominant weather often seems to be dreary, sometimes relentless, rain. That said, it's hard to beat a clear, frosty, winter's morning – which can appear anytime from Autumn. Snow, and the coldest temperatures, tend to feature from late December to February. And then there's Christmas which, notwithstanding the crass commercial aspects, is a special time for most people.

## December in Britain

**The Winter Solstice** – the shortest day and the longest night of the year, when the sun is lowest in the sky – takes place on or around 21st December. Thousands congregate at ancient sites, such as Stonehenge in Wiltshire, to welcome the rising sun.

**Christmas Eve**, 24th December, isn't a Bank Holiday, but many shops and businesses close early.

**Christmas Day**, 25th December, is a Bank Holiday in the UK – as is the following day, Boxing Day. If either or both days fall over a weekend, the Bank Holiday is carried forward to the next weekday.

**New Year's Eve**, 31st December, isn't a Bank Holiday, but many shops and businesses close early. New Year is generally celebrated around the country, with public celebrations in major cities, such as Edinburgh and London. Some of these events are ticket only, though of course fireworks can be observed from local viewpoints such as Primrose Hill in London or Calton Hill in Edinburgh.

**Allendale Baal Festival** - also known as the Tar Barl, Bah'l and Bahl, the Allendale Tar Bar'l is a more exclusive New Year event – a traditional fire festival, possibly originating in the middle ages. Key figures are 45 guisers, local men who carry whisky barrels filled with burning hot tar in a colourful procession through the town of Allendale, near Hexham.

**Stonehaven Fireballs Festival** allegedly has its roots in pagan traditions. Residents of this Aberdeenshire town parade along the High Street on Hogmanay, swinging giant fireballs to drive evil spirits away and purge the old year.

## January in Britain

**New Year's Day**, 1st January, is a Bank Holiday in the UK. 2nd January is also a Scottish Bank Holiday.

**Up Helly Aa** – the famous Up Helly Aa fire festival held in Lerwick, Shetland, Scotland, to mark the end of the Yule season, takes place on the last Tuesday in January. The festival involves a torchlit procession by squads of costumed participants (known as guisers) that culminate in the burning of Viking galley. The celebration is said to have developed from a tradition of tar barrelling.

**Burns' Night** on 25th January celebrates the Scottish poet's birthday in 1759. Dine on haggis, neeps and tatties, washed down with whisky. Events are by no means limited to Scotland and it is common to host a Burns' Supper at home.

**Chinese New Year.** Chinese New Year falls during late January-early February. Parades and celebrations take place in many UK cities, such as Liverpool and Manchester, though the largest is usually in London.

## February in Britain

**Valentine's Day** – 14th February is St Valentine's Day. Valentine might have been more than one person, but is generally considered to be the patron saint of lovers, epileptics, and beekeepers.

**The Brit Awards** – the British record industry's annual popular music awards take place in mid-February. You can't go unless you're invited – but it is normally on TV.

**Shropshire Day** – 23rd February (the feast day of St Milburga), celebrating the county sometimes abbreviated to 'Salop'. Shropshire's county town is Shrewsbury.

Finally, in February you should spot some snowdrops; a sign that spring is just around the corner and life begins again.

# ABOUT THE AUTHOR

Mike Biles was born and grew up in England. He studied medieval and modern British and European history at university and was planning on teaching it. Instead, he moved to London (where the streets are paved with gold) and drifted into a career running his own business, undertaking planning and managing projects for business clients. Mostly a lover of Britain and often at his happiest with his nose in a history book, or exploring a historic site where the past is close, several years ago Mike began a blog – now an increasingly authoritative website – 'A Bit About Britain' - https://bitaboutbritain.com/ . His first book, 'A Bit about Britain's History' is a by-product of the website, as is his second offering, 'A Bit About Britain's High Days and Holidays'.

Mike is married to someone and lives without any cats, dogs, or other pets, in a house in a village somewhere in Britain.

# A Bit About Britain's History
From a long time ago until quite recently
## By Mike Biles

A Bit About Britain's History does exactly what you think it should. It gives a brief account of Britain's amazing story, from a long time ago until quite recently, and is a perfect reminder of what you might have learned at school, as well as an introduction to one or two things you may never have heard before. Or perhaps you're coming to the subject fresh and want to understand a little of how Britain evolved. It is quite a tale, from man's first footsteps across a land that is now under the sea, to the digital age. Told through a few dozen short articles, A Bit About Britain's History explains the essentials of every period, including how the ancestors of the British arrived, how they fought each other, formed nations, fell out over religion, acquired a large empire, made things, became gradually more democratic, helped win a couple of world wars and were left wondering what to do next.

Included at the end of the book are detailed timelines for each period, which provide useful reference for all the important (and a few not so important) dates and events, and which also make fascinating reading in their own right.

A Bit About Britain's History might be the only book on British history you'll ever need; or it might be your stepping stone to more in-depth reading.

Find A Bit About Britain's History on an Amazon website near you, or ask your local bookshop, library, school and heritage attraction to stock it immediately.

Printed in Great Britain
by Amazon